DANCING IN THE RAIN

Finding Joy

in the

Midst of

the Storm

Cindy Shufflebarger

WinePress **WP** Publishing™

Unless otherwise noted, all Scriptures are taken from the *Holy Bible, New International Version*®, *NIV*®. Copyright © 1973, 1978, 1984 by Biblica, Inc.™ Used by permission of Zondervan. All rights reserved worldwide. WWW.ZONDERVAN.COM

Scripture references marked NKJV are taken from the *New King James Version*, © 1979, 1980, 1982 by Thomas Nelson, Inc., Publishers. Used by permission.

Scripture references marked NASB are taken from the *New American Standard Bible*, © 1960, 1963, 1968, 1971, 1972, 1973, 1975, 1977 by The Lockman Foundation. Used by permission.

Scripture references marked NLT are taken from the *Holy Bible, New Living Translation*, copyright © 1996, 2004 by Tyndale Charitable Trust. Used by permission of Tyndale House Publishers, Wheaton, Illinois 60189. All rights reserved.

Scripture references marked KJ21 are taken from *The Holy Bible, 21st Century King James Version* (KJ21®), Copyright © 1994, Deuel Enterprises, Inc., Gary, SD 57237, and used by permission.

ISBN 13: 978-1-57921-983-3
ISBN 10: 1-57921-983-7
Library of Congress Catalog Card Number: 2008933080

Shirley –
May you experience
an abundance of
His joy + love,
Cindy Shufflebarger

In memory of Ashlynn Faith,
a true gift and blessing

CONTENTS

Acknowledgments   vii

Preface   ix

Introduction   xi

Chapter One: What Is Joy?   1
Chapter Two: A Matter of Perspective   15
Chapter Three: Out of Control and Into the Arms of God   35
Chapter Four: God's Endless Love   47
Chapter Five: Your Relationship with God   57
Chapter Six: God Is Enough   77
Chapter Seven: Ask What, Not Why   99
Chapter Eight: Remembering God's Goodness   113
Chapter Nine: Reaping a Harvest   125
Chapter Ten: The Choice   137

Appendix   149

Endnotes   151

ACKNOWLEDGMENTS

To my friends, family and mentors who assisted in various ways—Thank you for the prayers, guidance, constructive feedback, and encouragement along the way.

To my children—Thank you for your patience as I was working on the book and for cheering me on with enthusiasm. I love you—every intricate and unique detail—and know God was smiling upon me when He brought each of you into my life.

To my husband, Scott—Thank you for your support in every way. Most of all, thank you for believing in me.

To the Giver of Life and Father of Compassion—I humbly say thank You. Thank You for sustaining me and bringing comfort. Thank You for Your wisdom and guidance while writing. May You alone be glorified in the pages within.

PREFACE

I thought I had my life all together. I had accomplished most of my childhood goals. I was married and had started a family. I had an advanced degree, experienced a successful career, and better yet, enjoyed working part-time and staying at home with my daughter. I had a home and a great network of friends. I'd had the opportunity to do some traveling and was generally healthy and happy. Yet something was clearly missing.

I had worked so hard to create this life for myself, but I still wasn't satisfied. I was restless and felt a void. I began to wonder, "Is this really what life is all about?" I was quite disappointed and found myself, even in the midst of supposed success, questioning my existence. Surely there was more to life.

I became a Christian as a child and had been attending church ever since. But sadly, that was the extent of my spiritual life. I started actively seeking God about the time I gave birth to my first child. However, it was more of a self-help program than a relationship with God. I wanted to be a better person, in particular a great mother and wife, but I still seemed to rely on my own strength and abilities. I didn't really know what it meant to have a personal relationship with Christ. Even though I prayed on a fairly regular basis, it felt as if my prayers just vanished into the air.

Fortunately, God started to tug at my heart and draw me nearer to Him. I was participating in a study called *Experiencing God,* and I had finally found the missing piece in my life—the source of true joy. And the more I experienced Him, the more I desired Him. However, what I was about to experience would send me flying out of control but exactly to the place where God wanted me.

As I share my journey, I pray that you will come to know God in a new and refreshing way and that you will see His glory revealed.

INTRODUCTION

In a perfect world, there would be no pain or suffering. Instead, we are surrounded by hurting people. Most of us are struggling right now with some sort of pain. If you find yourself in that place of darkness or continue to wrestle with past hurts, I pray that you will be encouraged by the pages that follow and that you'll see God's goodness and light.

In the chapters of this book, I share my experiences through the life and death of my daughter. There are several other angles I could have used to tell my story. I could have shared my experiences solely from the perspective of my grief or even entered a monologue about the collision of the medical world's view of life and mine. However, I've chosen to share my story from the perspective of my spiritual journey. Taking this approach has been a complete step of faith, because it requires a high level of transparency and the sharing of personal thoughts and experiences with the world around me. So why am I doing it? Because my hope is that others can experience God in some of the ways I have and discover the thrill of knowing that the all-powerful Creator of the universe loves you more than you can conceive. And so, I expose myself with the hope of spreading God's love to others. Once you've experienced it, you, too, will want others to know the same joy and reach their own victories.

A friend recently gave me a wall plaque that says, "Life isn't about waiting for the storm to pass, it's about learning to dance in the rain." Storms in life are inevitable, and they usually come unannounced and unwelcomed. If we spent all our time just waiting for the storms to pass, we'd miss a great deal of living. The principles I share throughout this book apply to any kind of storm in life. These are not sterile facts and formulas, but living and practical salve for the soul. Maybe you are in the middle of financial problems, marital problems, or struggles with health; God is ready and willing to help you weather the storm. The pages ahead point to the path of health and healing through a relationship with God. I don't pretend to know your struggles in life. I also won't compare mine with yours. I won't even promise the proverbial "quick fix." However, my hope is that by sharing my experiences you'll see the heart of God and how He works in the lives of those who love Him. I pray that you'll be drawn to God's love and strength as we embark on this journey together.

Please join me as my story begins . . .

"Mrs. Shufflebarger, your blood work suggests there may be a problem with your baby. There's a 30 percent chance your baby has trisomy 18. We'd like to see you on Monday for additional testing." I heard the words on a Friday night, but I decided not to worry over the weekend. In the meantime, I did a brief online search to learn about trisomy 18. *Surely, my baby doesn't really have this chromosomal defect,* I thought. *Babies with trisomy 18 don't live. I'm sure it was just a false positive that happens so frequently with these tests. But why would the doctor call me at 7:30 on a Friday night? I won't worry. I can't worry. It can't possibly be true. I'll have friends and family start praying, just to be safe.*

INTRODUCTION

As I lay in the dimly-lit room looking at the monitor, the ultrasound technician was quiet. I remember hearing faint sounds. I could hear the hum of the electronic equipment, the clicking as the technician typed, and the rustling of my husband's jacket as he shifted his weight. But mostly I heard silence. I couldn't take the silence. My mind was screaming, *Talk to me!* I needed some information. Having had two children already, I'd seen enough ultrasound pictures to have a vague idea of what I was seeing on the screen. I saw a heart—a beating heart. Good. But why did the technician look so serious? She kept studying the heart. *I can't take it. I need to know.* As I started probing for information, she began to share what she was looking for and called the neonatologist into the room.

"We're 99 percent sure the baby has trisomy 18. It has a major defect in the heart, cysts on the brain, and hands and feet that are indicative of trisomy 18. We can do an amniocentesis to be certain, but I'm confident this is trisomy 18. It's early enough in the pregnancy that you still have options."

Options? I don't want options. I want my baby! We somehow conveyed to the doctor that we wanted to continue the pregnancy. "Mrs. Shufflebarger, the baby won't live. It most likely won't even be born alive. You have options that can spare you a lot of pain." I was trying to process the shocking news and still communicate the message that we did not want to terminate the pregnancy.

She's talking about my baby. She keeps calling the baby "it." I can't move. I can barely breathe. Lord, help me!

"Maybe you should take some time to think about it. I'm so sorry. And oh, it's a girl."

I have no recollection of telling my parents the news or of what my children were doing when I returned home. I vaguely remember the drive home—mostly that I was alone in the car because my husband had come straight from work to meet me at the doctor's appointment. I think I was numb. It was all very surreal. There were lots of tears and my mind was cluttered. I couldn't think clearly; my thoughts ran wild. *How did I get to this place in my life? What is God doing? How will I survive? How will this affect my kids? What do I tell them? What are we going to do? Will she be born alive? Do I plan a funeral? Will I get to meet her?*

Dear God, please let me hold her. My heart aches for this child as my dreams for her are dashed. I desperately want to hold my baby alive. I beg you, Lord. I need a miracle!

*You turned my wailing into dancing; you removed
my sackcloth and clothed me with joy,
that my heart may sing to you and not be silent.*

O LORD my God, I will give you thanks forever.

—Psalm 30:11–12

Chapter One

WHAT IS JOY?

*I*t's New Year's Day, and as I reflect on the past year, I realize I have choices to make. Tough choices. You see, a few months ago I experienced the birth and death of my third child. So now, I can either choose to rejoice in the Lord or sit and wallow in my grief. I'm torn. Part of me wants to rejoice because against all odds, Ashlynn was born alive, and I was granted two and a half wonderful days to hold and love and care for my sweet baby girl; however, my natural tendency is to want to sit in the midst of my "mud puddle" and cry. I would love to crawl back into bed, pull the covers over my head, and sleep my pain away. My family has been turned upside down. My other children are grieving and suffering. My marriage has been strained. My parents and other family members think I should be finished grieving and moving on with my life. Most people don't know what to say to me, so they don't say anything at all. I feel all alone. Painfully alone. Yet, I still feel a sense of hope . . . .

Pain and suffering are universal. They need no definition. Instantly, hundreds of examples come to mind. Whether it is divorce, the loss of a job, abuse, the loss of a loved one, terminal illness, struggles with addiction, or anything else on a long

1

list, suffering is all around us. If it's not directly impacting our lives at this very moment, it's affecting someone we know. Yes, everyone can identify with pain and suffering.

Joy, however, is a different story.

What comes to mind when you think of joy? That which brings joy to one may not bring joy to another. Similarly, what causes joy in your life can change depending on your present circumstances and the stage in life in which you find yourself. The things that brought you joy as a child aren't the same things that bring joy as you grow and mature. Likewise, when the newness of some possession or relationship wears off, the joy often wanes as well. Think about your wants and desires over the past several years. Can you even remember what you wanted for Christmas or a birthday? If you can remember, does that gift still bring you the excitement it did when you first received it?

My children's responses to their holiday presents are the perfect example of this. How many Christmas gifts are still being played with by the middle of January? Many of those brand new toys—the items they simply had to have—are shelved. Then when those treasures are rediscovered later, the fun and excitement returns.

If we're honest with ourselves, aren't we a little like that, too? Unfortunately, our desires are often bigger and more expensive than children's Christmas toys. How many of us are still excited about that new car after owning it for a year or two, especially after the kids have spilled a few drinks on the seats and we've scuffed the paint on the doors. We may even find ourselves shopping around for a new vehicle within the first couple of years. Of course, we do this browsing under the guise of needing a safe, reliable vehicle with low miles so that nothing will happen to our precious family while we go about our daily business. If we're a little more disciplined, or simply strapped for money, we may forego actually shopping for a new car but still dream about it. Why? Because we've lost interest in the old one. The happiness we felt as a result of the newness of our perfectly good car is gone.

If you can't relate to the car example, maybe your hot button is jewelry or clothes or home décor. The point's still the same; the excitement over having something new wanes and with the exit of that excitement goes our joy. We invest tremendous amounts of time and energy on things of this world—things that have absolutely no impact on eternity—all to achieve some sense of immediate happiness or pleasure. What we are actually craving is joy.

But is it even possible to capture joy and hang on to it? By this, I mean, is there a true joy that is everlasting, or is joy always fleeting? I'd like to suggest to you that happiness is temporary, but joy is lasting. Let's explore the difference between happiness and joy.

According to the Merriam-Webster® Online Dictionary, happiness means "a state of well-being and contentment," or it can refer to "a pleasurable or satisfying experience."[1] In other words, happiness is based on experience or circumstances. When all is going well, we're happy. When things go awry, we're not happy.

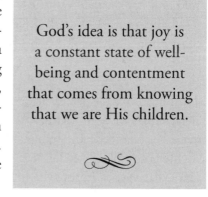

God's idea is that joy is a constant state of well-being and contentment that comes from knowing that we are His children.

Joy is defined as a synonym for happiness[2]; however, the joy I refer to in the remainder of this book is not the same as the dictionary's definition. This joy is much more. It is not a wavering emotion. Instead, God's idea is that joy is a constant state of well-being and contentment that comes from knowing that we are His children. It is not dependent on our circumstances. This definition may require a slight shift in your thinking, but please stay with me. Discovering this joy is worth the journey.

Finding Joy

To find joy, we need only to look toward God. True joy comes from God. As we walk with Him, we come to know Him as our provider, healer, protector, comforter, redeemer, and Father. Having a relationship with the God who is all these things and more is the key to joy. Any upset He comforts. Any need He provides. Any disease He handles, and so on. As our eyes focus on Him and our hearts tune in to His, we're able to see things from a different perspective. Believe it or not, it's even possible for God to break through with a supply of joy despite the most devastating of circumstances.

Ashlynn's death has been the most painful loss I've ever experienced. Words cannot convey the depths of my sorrow and pain. My security vanished. Every belief I held about God was challenged. Most of all, I feel a gaping void in my life that seems impossible to fill. My heart aches.

I was helpless as I watched my baby fight for her life and take her last breath. All I could do was hold her and love her. Nothing in my life will ever be the same again. Relationships have changed. My thoughts and beliefs have changed. My self-image has changed. The image others have of me has changed. My life is completely redefined.

Not a day goes by in which I don't think of Ashlynn and long for her. Almost everything stimulates thoughts of her. The same holds true for my oldest daughter. She is painfully aware of her sister's absence. She watches another baby being passed around at a church supper and whispers to me, "I wish Ashlynn were still here." We drive by the hospital on a routine errand and she emphatically says, "Why do we have to go this way? Seeing the hospital makes me miss Ashlynn." Not only do I deal with my own grief, I deal with the anguish of knowing my other children hurt. And again, I feel helpless. I can't chase our pain away.

Trying to face this pain on my own just wasn't working, and somehow I needed to redirect my thoughts. I couldn't go on without changing my perspective, but I didn't want to dishonor Ashlynn's memory, either. I couldn't just stop thinking about her. I also couldn't just erase my daughter's thoughts and hurt over losing her little sister. The only thing I could think to do—the one thing that had to work—was to exercise complete faith and trust in God. Even though I

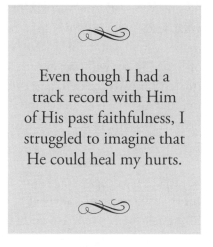

Even though I had a track record with Him of His past faithfulness, I struggled to imagine that He could heal my hurts.

had a track record with Him of His past faithfulness, I struggled to imagine that He could heal my hurts. I determined to let Him have a go of it. What other choice did I really have? My perspective shift consisted of continuing through the maze of sorrow (which I couldn't escape anyway) while holding the Master's hand.

I am respectfully inviting you to travel with me as we discuss getting through the painful maze of whatever sorrow has touched your life. Perhaps you haven't experienced the death of a child, but maybe you've lost a job and thus financial security. Or maybe you're going through a divorce and feel all alone. Whatever trial or hardship, I hope you'll join me on the journey to finding joy.

So how do we start to change the way we view uncomfortable, devastating, even tragic events? And furthermore, how is it possible to find joy when life seems like a disaster?

Let's begin by thinking about what God has done already. First of all, He loves us so much that He sent His Son to save us from our sins. He gave us the gift of salvation—eternal life—not because we deserve it, but simply because He loves us. Think about it: eternal life in the presence of God. There will be no more suffering or pain or sorrow . . . forever! And look what Jesus willingly gave up to become the sacrificial lamb that makes this possible for us. Not only did He endure every type of hardship we will ever experience, but He was also ridiculed, treated unjustly, beaten, and murdered in the most horrifying manner anyone could imagine. He gave up His glorious life in heaven to come to earth to be tortured for us. All of that blows my mind.

In his book, *Ninety Minutes in Heaven*, Don Piper shares that he experienced heaven. He says his time there was so wonderful that when he was revived here on earth, he was essentially homesick for heaven. He endured many torturous months of recovery, and the years that followed remained painful and always a struggle.

I often wonder if that's how Jesus felt while here on earth. Did He just want to go home? Yet, because He knew it was His Father's will for Him to be here carrying out the mission of our salvation, He lovingly endured every moment. What an amazing gift and testament of His love for us!

What else has God already done? Not only did God send His Son to die in our place because we're sinful, but think about what God has saved us from. In the book of Revelation, we're told that if our name is not written in the book of life, we'll be thrown into the fiery lake of burning sulfur (20:15). I don't know about you, but I'm not interested in taking a swim in any fiery lake. Think about your most painful experience then multiply that by a million. Now, imagine enduring it forever. Whatever the magnitude, that is not even close to the horrors of what hell will be like. I don't think we can humanly understand how torturous hell will be, but we don't have to worry. By choosing to rely on what Christ has done, we receive His love and mercy, and an eternal stint in hell is no longer in our future. We will be heirs of God and co-heirs with Christ in heaven. That's pretty amazing.

That leads us to look at one other provision God has made for us. He has loved us enough to send His Son; He has made it possible for us to miss hell; and now third, He has provided heaven. Although heaven may be hard to imagine, God's Word gives us glimpses into what to expect.

Heaven is greater than anything here on earth. The Bible says that no eye has seen, no ear has heard, and no mind has even conceived what God has prepared for those who love Him (1 Cor. 2:9). We're told of streets of gold, a sea of crystal, an array of jewels, mansions prepared by the King, perfect fellowship with other believers, and eternity in the presence of God. There is no darkness and there are no tears, pain, or sorrow. It is sheer perfection. Our human, finite minds cannot even fathom how wondrous heaven truly is. Those in the Bible who've given accounts of their visions of heaven struggle with their descriptions because there aren't human words to describe it; however, heaven is a real place, and those who are believers in Christ will spend eternity there. Our joy and satisfaction will finally be complete!

Filled with Joy

Recognizing what God has already done for us, don't we have adequate reason to be filled with joy? God's promises far outweigh any pain and suffering we endure in this life. Additionally, we're told that man's days are but a handbreadth, the span of our years is nothing before God, and "each man's life is but a breath" (Ps. 39:5). Simply put, we're here for the blink of an eye. Our suffering in this world is miniscule compared to eternity.

Please know that I'm not trying to diminish your current pain or struggles; however, I'm trying to put them in perspective and make them more bearable. If this life is but a split second and we know we have an eternity in heaven to look forward to, we can experience God's joy while we're here, even if we're hurting. Even if you're not yet convinced, please keep reading. My hope is to help you set your eyes and your heart on eternal things. With the right focus, the trials of this world can fade into the background.

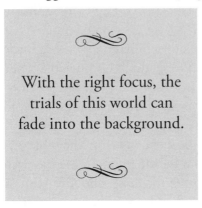

With the right focus, the trials of this world can fade into the background.

The psalmist writes "My soul shall be joyful in the LORD; it shall rejoice in His salvation" (Ps. 35:9 NKJV). Even in the midst of his trials, the writer chose to focus on the promise of salvation. And that's the key: where we place our focus is a choice. Joy is a choice.

Our human minds and bodies want immediate relief from whatever is causing discomfort. It takes a great deal of effort to stay focused on God and His promises. That's why it's so important to stay immersed in the Word every day. Reading and re-reading God's promises is the only way to stay focused on them. They must become the forefront of our thoughts instead of the external pressures that surround us. We're reminded in 2 Corinthians 10:5 to take captive every thought to make it obedient to Christ. It's easy to be overrun with thoughts and emotion, especially in the midst of trying times. Our pain and grief consume us, ruling our thoughts and actions, and warping our sense of reality. These are the times when it's especially important to turn to God's Word for truth. Otherwise, we begin to believe the lies that Satan tries to present.

After Ashlynn's death, I battled thoughts such as, *If God loved me, He would have healed her.* I was letting my thoughts and feelings distort truth. Although that statement felt like the truth, it wasn't. That thought sprang from my pain. The truth was that God's love for me was demonstrated at the cross. Good things that happened to me were not proof of His love, nor were bad things that happened to me proof that He didn't love me. The ups and downs of life are not a barometer for His proven love for me. God's Word says He is the same yesterday, today, and forever (Heb. 13:8). Since that's true, God's love didn't change when Ashlynn died. The more I pored over His Word, the more I was repeatedly reminded of His love for me and I was able to take captive the distorted thoughts that challenged the truth.

Are you struggling to accept God's truths for your life? Do you believe the lie that you're inferior because your home or your car or your clothes aren't as nice as those of your coworkers? The truth is that you were created in the image of God, and His love for you is infinite. Or perhaps you believe the lie that God could never forgive you and therefore you are bound by the chains of guilt that rob you of all joy. The truth is that the Bible tells us that God will forgive our sins and make all things new.

Consider this, too, "We have this treasure in jars of clay to show that this all-surpassing power is from God and not from us. We are hard pressed on every side, but not crushed; perplexed, but not in despair; persecuted, but not abandoned; struck down, but not destroyed" (2 Cor. 4:7–9). The treasure within us is not our own personal strength. As Christians, we are filled with the Holy Spirit. "The fruit of the Spirit is love, *joy,* peace, patience, kindness, goodness, faithfulness, gentleness and self-control" (Gal. 5:22–23, emphasis added). So you see, because of the Holy Spirit's residence within us, we're also filled with everything He is, i.e., with each element of the fruit. We are filled with joy. If we allow the Holy Spirit to work in us even at times of crisis and sorrow, joy can flow from within. God gave us free will and He doesn't make us submit to Him; however, if we will only hand Him our grief and let Him do what He does—operate as Lord of our lives—amazing things will happen.

Maintaining Joy

We don't just magically find joy one day and remain joyful for the rest of our lives. Prayer helps us stay on course. When pain seems to be overtaking us, it's easy to look at someone else's life and judge their circumstances as "greener pastures."

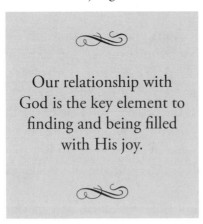

Our relationship with God is the key element to finding and being filled with His joy.

Talking with God focuses our minds and hearts on eternal things. Redirecting our eyes toward Him helps us center on the reality that greener pastures are just an illusion. We wouldn't be happy there either. We'll only find joy if we stick to God and what He has planned for us. Comparing ourselves to others is futile.

This is where prayer enters the picture. We have to be close to God to know what He has planned. And we can only get close by reading His Word and praying. Our relationship with God is the key element to finding and being filled with His joy.

10

So you see, our identity in Christ is the only way to be filled with joy at all times. Consider all that Paul, the apostle, endured. We're told that he was beaten, imprisoned, shipwrecked, and slandered; yet, he was able to continue his passionate service for Christ. Why? Because his joy wasn't based on his circumstances or anything external. Paul's joy was based on his relationship and hope in Christ.

In the midst of struggles or persecution, we need to remind ourselves that we are children of God. It is that foundation that keeps us from being tossed around in the storms of life. He is the rock—our stability and security. Just like Paul, whose sense of self was grounded in Christ, we can be filled with joy regardless of feelings or circumstances. However, it requires training, discipline, and the grace of God.

Throughout the remainder of this book, I'll share my journey and the gems that God revealed to me through my daughter Ashlynn's life and death. We'll dig deeper into finding joy and being filled with it. As you read on, remember that God often whispers to us while the rest of the world screams. Don't let the many distractions of this world steal your joy. Turn to God to hear His healing whispers. The reward is great and He will fill you with great joy.

God Says:

- "The ransomed of the LORD will return. They will enter Zion with singing; everlasting joy will crown their heads. Gladness and joy will overtake them, and sorrow and sighing will flee away" (Isa. 51:11).
- "Those who sow in tears will reap with songs of joy. He who goes out weeping, carrying seed to sow, will return with songs of joy, carrying sheaves with him" (Ps. 126:5–6).

11

- "You have made known to me the path of life; you fill me with joy in your presence, with eternal pleasures at your right hand" (Ps. 16:11).
- "You turned my wailing into dancing; you removed my sackcloth and clothed me with joy, that my heart may sing to you and not be silent. O LORD my God, I will give you thanks forever" (Ps. 30:11–12).
- "Restore to me the joy of your salvation" (Ps. 51:12).
- "My lips will shout for joy when I sing praise to you—I, whom you have redeemed" (Ps. 71:23).
- "Yet I will rejoice in the LORD, I will be joyful in God my Savior" (Hab. 3:18).
- "Be joyful always; pray continually; give thanks in all circumstances, for this is God's will for you in Christ Jesus" (1 Thess. 5:16–18).
- "Let us fix our eyes on Jesus, the author and perfecter of our faith, who for the joy set before him endured the cross, scorning its shame, and sat down at the right hand of the throne of God. Consider him who endured such opposition from sinful men, so that you will not grow weary and lose heart" (Heb. 12:2–3).
- "May the God of hope fill you with all joy and peace as you trust in him, so that you may overflow with hope by the power of the Holy Spirit" (Rom. 15:13).

Your Chance to Dance:

- Think about what Jesus did for you at the cross and take time to thank God for the gift of salvation. Start your day by saying a prayer of thanksgiving.
- Post one or more of the verses above in visible places around you—on your bathroom mirror, on your refrigerator, in your day planner, at your computer, on the sun

visor of your car, etc. Immerse yourself in God's Word and begin to commit some of these verses to memory.

- *Jesus, Others, You*—in that order—spell *joy.* Think of ways to orient your life so that you put Jesus first and others next. What can you commit to do for Jesus today? Who has a need that you can help meet? Make a list and get busy focusing on kingdom work. The result will be joy in your heart.

- Learn about heaven. There are some great Scripture-based books on heaven. Better yet, read what the Bible has to say about heaven and fix your eyes on eternity.

Note: If you don't know Jesus as your personal Lord and Savior, or if you're uncertain about your salvation, turn to the Appendix at the end of this book to learn more.

Chapter Two

A MATTER OF
PERSPECTIVE

As I reflect on the past year, I can say that my daughter's life was much too short. She only lived two-and-a-half days. What a sad story. Or I can think of the same experience and come to the conclusion that God granted us two-and-a-half incredible days with our beloved daughter and that I learned a lifetime of lessons from her. I can rejoice in the profound impact that she has had on my life and see that she fulfilled God's purpose for her life. What an amazing thing that her life accomplished so much in such a short time! I can only hope that I can positively affect someone in the same way that she has blessed my life. The latter is the path I've chosen, and it has given me a great sense of joy to have been Ashlynn's mother.

Have you ever gone out in the rain and just stood, letting the drops fall upon your face? As adults, most of us dodge the rain. Whether we're making a mad dash to the car or covering our heads with an umbrella at the first sign of a sprinkle, we often take great measures to stay dry. Most children I've observed, however, tend to take their time in the rain. They look around, step or hop in puddles, and generally seem to enjoy being in the rain. They might look up while holding out their hands, catching the raindrops. They may even stick out their tongues, hoping some drops will plop in their mouth. In any case, children usually are not in any hurry to take cover.

As I thought about this, I tried to determine when I changed from enjoying playing in the rain to avoiding it at all costs. I can't define a specific moment that the transformation occurred, but it certainly happened when I wasn't looking. I can remember the enjoyment of playing soccer in the rain in high school. It was refreshing, albeit messy, to feel the cool drops plummeting around me; however, off the soccer field, I wouldn't want to be caught out in the rain—it might mess up my hair.

After an emotionally and physically challenging year, January first rolled around and I decided I should experience dancing in the rain. What a perfect way to start the year. I found my coat and ventured out onto our deck to stand in the rain. I felt a little silly at first. My head entertained the thought, *the neighbors are going to think I've lost my mind*; nevertheless, I stood there, barefoot, soaking in the rain. The sound of the falling drops was soothing, the feeling invigorating. Slowly I raised my face to the sky, closed my eyes, and allowed the cool drops to gently splash on my forehead, eyelids, and cheeks.

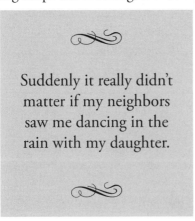

Suddenly it really didn't matter if my neighbors saw me dancing in the rain with my daughter.

My husband declined the offer to join me; however, my five-year-old daughter was quick to recognize this outing as the best idea I'd had in a long time. She donned her coat and joined me. Uninhibited, she immediately began to enjoy her time in the rain. She danced, spun, splashed, laughed, and had a blast. I gradually loosened up and joined her dance. Suddenly it really didn't matter if my neighbors saw me dancing in the rain with my daughter. I enjoyed myself that morning and found myself thanking God for rain, glorious rain.

An hour later, my husband received a trouble call from work and was forced to go out into the rain. I couldn't pass up the opportunity to chide him, pointing out that he should have gone out willingly when I invited him instead of having God find a way to make him go out into the wet weather. He wasn't convinced of God's participation in my example and remained annoyed for having to get wet.

This was all a matter of perspective. I chose to go out in the rain for the purpose of having fun. My husband didn't have a choice and would not be enjoying himself.

Not only is rain great fun to play in, but it's also necessary for life. Although we often look negatively at the rain, with it comes new life, refreshment, rainbows, and a reprieve from the scorching heat of summer days. As with rain on the earth, trials and hardships sometimes shower down and can produce growth—often in unexpected ways. Our perspective makes all the difference. The Bible tells us, "Suffering produces perseverance; perseverance, character; and character, hope. And hope does not disappoint us, because God has poured out his love into our hearts by the Holy Spirit, whom he has given us" (Rom. 5:3–5). As we grow in our belief of this truth, we'll embrace challenges and trials and look for what we can learn through them instead of becoming angry and bitter.

Expectations

Think about the many disappointments in life. Aren't they usually a result of unmet expectations? Whether you envisioned your role as a grandparent in a different way, you expected you'd live a certain lifestyle, or you expected that your child would be perfectly healthy; it's easy to be let down when things don't turn out as expected. Whether we're let down because of our own choices or because God has other plans, we're faced with a critical decision when we experience disappointment. We can complain, cry, whine, be stoic, depressed, and just plain miserable; or we can choose to readjust our thinking and look for the good in the situation. Just think: we may be missing out on a blessing because it was packaged differently than what we expected. I'm not suggesting that we ignore our feelings of grief or loss, but that we not get stuck in those emotions. At some point, with God's help, we need to turn our tragedies into triumphs by looking for the possible good in each situation.

Neither my husband nor I planned for or expected it when he was laid off from his job. It happened without warning, and we were shocked. He was not given a severance package, I was only working part-time, and we were already stretched financially. Needless to say, this stressful situation ushered in a challenging time that required a great deal of reliance on God.

Ten weeks later when my husband secured a job that seemed like a reasonable opportunity, he quickly discovered the job was not what he expected. The company was in financial trouble and he rarely was paid on time. The job came with many other stresses and hardships, too. He struggled there through a painful year of uncertainties.

Finally, our circumstances seemed to brighten when my husband was presented with the opportunity to purchase a company in his field of expertise. Although all uncertainties would not disappear, this was a much more stable situation. In hindsight, the experiences my husband encountered were the best preparation for that which was in his future. The layoff and miserable job that followed painted a very clear picture of how not to run a business. He never would have learned what he did had he not experienced those challenges and trials. His unexpected disappointment turned out to be a blessing, but it took time and some suffering to discover it.

Likewise, the people in Jesus' time had expectations about who the Messiah would be. They expected a mighty warrior king as their almighty Savior. Instead, Jesus came in the form of a baby, born to a family with very modest means. He lived a perfect life void of physical violence and with little fanfare. Jesus was bold in His words but gentle and loving in demeanor. Because He did not meet the people's expectation of a king, they eventually crucified Him. It wasn't until His death and resurrection that many had the vision to see Him for who He really was.

It's hard to imagine that a death, divorce, or abuse could turn out to be a blessing. And maybe the loss or event itself is not a blessing. But painful circumstances can produce growth that leads to good. Sadly, we often overlook opportunities for great joy because we're too busy being disap-

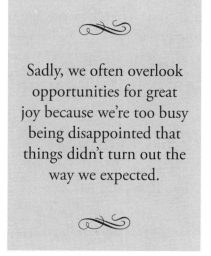

Sadly, we often overlook opportunities for great joy because we're too busy being disappointed that things didn't turn out the way we expected.

pointed that things didn't turn out the way we expected. I never expected that I would experience the death of a child. And had I started grieving Ashlynn's death when we learned of her condition (seventeen weeks into the pregnancy), I would never have experienced the joy of her life. It's hard to even articulate how much I love her and how she has forever changed my life for the better. Her life and death drew me closer to God and I experienced Him in ways I'd never known before. Her life taught me how special but fragile each life is. She inspired me to do new things and stop living life inside my comfort zone. It continues to amaze me that someone whose life only lasted two-and-a-half days is making an impact on my daily thoughts and decisions.

I could have wandered down the path of bitterness and despair. Instead, by the grace of God, I've chosen a different perspective. I have very warm thoughts of Ashlynn, and she'll forever share a very special piece of my heart. Did I expect the pain and heartbreak that was ahead when I discovered I was pregnant? Absolutely not. Did I have any idea what a blessing her physically deformed and weak body could have had on my life? Never. I'm still in awe. But one thing's for sure, she was the unexpected blessing of a lifetime and I am forever grateful. My time with her and the love I have for her far outweigh the pain I've experienced.

Ultimately, I have to trust not only that He can see the bigger picture, but also that His plan is better than mine.

God's Word states that He wants to give us immeasurably more than we could ever ask or imagine (Eph. 3:20). If God wants to give us more than we're asking for, it just makes sense to accept it. Of course, this means exercising a willingness to let go of our own desires or even change our thinking in order to take hold of God's plan. Ultimately, I have to trust not only that He can see the bigger picture, but also that His plan is better than mine.

At Christmas, my two-year-old decided she wanted a Hello Kitty® spinning toothbrush. That's all she wanted. And that's all she'd tell Santa she wanted. Her mind was set on a Hello Kitty® toothbrush. This was probably the easiest Christmas request she'd ever make and it's no surprise that her wish was granted. However, we had more in mind for her. We wanted her to have a kid-sized trampoline, partly because she likes to watch too much TV and it would provide some physical activity, but more importantly because we thought it would be fun for her. But then came the task of subtly convincing her that the trampoline was what *she* wanted. We never did convince her of it. On Christmas morning, she was just as elated about the Hello Kitty® toothbrush as she was about the trampoline.

Just as I had desired something greater for my daughter than a toothbrush, God has great things planned for us. By walking in His will and being open to His plans, we can experience His full blessing. He has a purpose in mind which we may not understand, but we can rest assured knowing that if we're in a right relationship with Him, He has big things ahead. Although those blessings may not come as we expect, they will surely come. Are you willing to wait expectantly for what He has planned for you? Can you trust that He will sustain you and walk with you through the sometimes painful journey?

God's View, Not Ours

Somewhere along the way, our society became one that learned to expect the best of everything. We began to think that we're entitled to an easy and comfortable life. (Perhaps when we asked for a toothbrush, we got a trampoline, too.) Look down the aisles of most bookstores and you'll find an array of titles that promise success, wealth, good looks, good health, etc. These books sell a "feel good" attitude that we deserve the best and that by employing the right formula, the best is available. However, the reality is that God doesn't promise us a life that is always positive and free from pain and suffering. On the contrary, we're told that as Christians, we'll encounter persecution for our beliefs (2 Tim. 3:12). God even told Paul, His faithful servant, that his pain was being allowed to keep him humble (2 Cor. 12:7). God did assure Paul, though, that His grace was all he needed to handle it.

DANCING IN THE RAIN

Unfortunately for us, we exhibit very little patience for pain and hard times. We do not always choose to acknowledge God's possible hand in the matter, so subsequently our view of Him often changes depending on our circumstances.

How often do we sing His praises while all is great, and immediately start to grumble and question Him when things get a little uncomfortable? Are you angry with God because your marriage failed? Are you upset with Him because you didn't get the promotion you wanted? Our emotional pain dulls our memory of the fact that God always stays the same. His love is steadfast. His sovereignty is never ending. God tells us that His thoughts and ways are different than ours (Isa. 55:8). We will never fully understand God and his infinite wisdom, but we still need to trust Him. God can certainly handle our anger, but when we stay angry with God, we're the ones missing out.

When we're faced with a difficult situation, it is helpful to try to view it from God's perspective or at least in context of eternal value. God uses trials in our lives for many reasons. For example, He could be trying to get our attention, to draw us closer to Himself, to discipline us, to teach us, to draw others to Him, or to prepare us for some other role. We can't possibly know all the reasons for hardships in our life, but as Christians, we are assured that in all things God works for the good of those who love Him and are called to His purpose (Rom. 8:28). In other words, God works things out for good for those who are a part of His kingdom. God sees the big picture, and we have to trust that He knows what He's doing even if it doesn't make sense to us. After all, we're here to complete God's work. This life, even our own life, is not about us.

I will never know God's purpose for Ashlynn's death. And, if given the choice, I'd still ask for a "do-over"—that He would have allowed her to live instead of die. However, I've accepted her death as part of His will and can now see many of the ways that God is using my pain and suffering for good. I have a deeper relationship with my husband and kids. I talk more to my children about eternal things instead of the temporal. I have a greater level of compassion for those who are hurting. I've been able to show God's love to others in ways I would have never dreamed of before now.

Are there ways you can use your struggles and hurts to share God's love with others? It is an honor for God to use you for His purposes. I encourage you to start asking Him to show you His view of your circumstances. Be bold and ask Him to use your past and present hurts to help others. I guarantee you'll delight in seeing Him glorified.

Focus on God Instead of Circumstances

Our focus is a determining factor in how well we deal with adversity. I used to pass out whenever I had blood drawn. Fortunately, I've learned how to prevent that from happening. It helps if I lie down, but the most effective technique is for the phlebotomist to walk me through the process of visual imagery. I'm told to pick a visual focal point on the wall and then I'm asked about a favorite place or vacation spot. I imagine that I'm there by talking through what I see, hear, and feel. As I describe this magnificent place, I'm so focused on it

Our focus is a determining factor in how well we deal with adversity.

that I barely realize that I've been stuck with a needle and blood is being drawn. It works; it's all about the focus.

You may be thinking, "That's great, but you're talking about a quick needle stick, not the pain I'm suffering." Perhaps a better analogy is the Lamaze technique used to manage labor pains.

It, too, is all about focus. Each time a woman feels a labor pain coming on, she's instructed to concentrate on controlled breathing. As the pain becomes more acute, her attention to her focal point is to become more intensified.

This physical pain-relief principle works the same with emotional sorrow. Focusing on God can give great relief during times of pain. What we're really doing is focusing on God's truth instead of relying on our senses. Our feelings aren't always the truth, and I think it's dangerous to trust our feelings when we're in the midst of hardships.

Our feelings are very complex and based on many factors: our interpretation of events and circumstances, past experiences, thoughts, beliefs, and even hormones. For example,

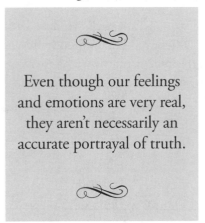

Even though our feelings and emotions are very real, they aren't necessarily an accurate portrayal of truth.

I've watched two family members, who were present for the same weekend event, give conflicting accounts of the details. They were both in the same room, heard the same discussions, and observed the same behaviors, but they interpreted the events very differently because of the subjectivity of feelings and emotions.

My point is that our perception of reality can be an illusion. Even though our feelings and emotions are very real, they aren't necessarily an accurate portrayal of truth, and therefore, we shouldn't always trust that what we're feeling is reality.

I can easily let my thoughts run wild until they escalate to the point of my being upset—all because of some imagined scenario. Have you ever faced a difficult meeting or perhaps a family gathering where there are interesting dynamics? You get yourself worked up beforehand because you conjured up notions of strife and conflict.

Our thoughts and emotions are very powerful; therefore, we need to be careful about letting them wander. The Bible tells us to take captive every thought for Christ (2 Cor. 10:5). What great advice that is! When we focus on our hurts over and over, it's difficult to heal. When we focus on God, we can move closer to Him and thus experience His healing salve each step of the way. As the old hymn says, all the troubles of this world fade away as we turn our eyes toward Jesus.[1]

When we focus on our hurts over and over, it's difficult to heal.

How do we focus on God? Spending time with Him in prayer, reading the Bible, singing praise music, reading biblically based books of encouragement, and choosing to saturate our thoughts with Him instead of our problems will ensure that we experience a liberating shift in our focus.

When times are tough, try looking up instead of down. This may sound like a cliché, but looking to God is your best chance for finding comfort, hope, and peace. As He sheds light on a situation, your chances are much greater that you'll see the truth—the truth that you're a child of God and that He loves you. Ask Him to reveal the truth. His Word tells us that He has no greater joy than to know that His children are walking in the truth (1 John 4). He can give help, guidance, comfort, and strength through His revelation of the truth.

Take a Walk in Someone Else's Shoes

The first Christmas after Ashlynn's death was very difficult. As I watched everyone shopping for their children, the void I felt was even more acute. Instead of searching for just the right present for my new baby girl, my big wish was that her gravestone would arrive before Christmas. Instead of her sitting in a bouncy seat near the tree on Christmas morning, her picture hung in an ornament hanging on the tree. I felt very isolated, and friends and family were all busy with their own lives. It seemed like no one was concerned. *How could everyone have forgotten already?* I thought. *Don't they know how much pain I'm in? Does anyone even care?*

When we're in the midst of a crisis, we often switch into survival mode, just trying to accomplish the necessary tasks of living. We take a few steps forward and then for whatever reason, we step back into the darkness. Self-pity creeps in. We may get grumpy. We may become depressed. We may start questioning God again.

I began wallowing in self-pity. I prayed that God would help me let go of those feelings and do something more productive. I wasn't aware what was happening at the time, but God put it on my heart to reach out to someone else—someone who had different struggles. I had been so consumed by my pain and suffering that it really hadn't occurred to me that others were suffering. God nudged me to step out of my comfort zone and give the gift of love. This was a huge step for me—a definite leap of faith.

I "just happened" to run into a family from church one day at the library. The mom was there with her two homeschooled daughters and her preschool son, Nico, who has Down syndrome. In the middle of my self-pity party that day, I started wondering about the challenges they faced. What was it like to live daily with a child who was "different" and had special needs? My daughter had special needs, but I only experienced taking care of those needs for a brief time. What if it had been for a lifetime? How would I have coped? Would people have turned their heads and tried not to look at her differences, or would they have seen her for the beautiful creation that she was? Would she have been invited to play dates and parties? Would people have volunteered to babysit? What would it have been like for us?

Those reflective questions caused me to realize that for most of my life I had been uncomfortable around those who had disabilities and special needs. I never thought less of them; I just wasn't sure what to say or do, so my insecurities led to avoidance. I suddenly understood why people responded to me as they did as I went through my grief. They simply didn't know what to say or do so they avoided me, or at least they avoided the topic of grieving and my daughter. As all those thoughts played out in my head, God was nudging me to reach out and take a giant leap out of my comfort zone.

I called and invited our young friend, Nico, to go to story time with us at the library. I think his mother thought I had lost my mind. She repeatedly cautioned that it would be hard work to have her son along and she basically tried to talk me out of taking him. Honestly, she scared me to death! I was already nervous and she was essentially telling me that I had good reason to be. I prayed a lot for the entire week before the outing.

The big day arrived. I picked Nico up, we visited the library, and we made it back to his house without incident. What a relief! I committed to coming back the next week, and we continued our visits for several months as he joined my daughter and me on our library jaunts. Was it always easy? No. But it was always worth it. He is helpful, sweet, and very funny. He is a spirited young boy who likes to have fun, much like other little boys. My heart warms to see him smile, even when it's a playful grin and I know it means that a chase is about to ensue. I have truly been blessed by getting to know our friend Nico.

The pain I experienced with Ashlynn's death made me stop and think about others. She gave me a new perspective on life and its value. Seeing the world from someone else's perspective is both a learning experience and a blessing.

As we progress through any kind of challenge, self-reflection and evaluation are important so that we recognize when we're backsliding into less productive thoughts and actions. The old adage, "one step forward, two steps back" can happen quickly, so it's important to take action immediately upon noticing slippage. Pray, asking God to help you look outside of yourself and your circumstances. There are others around us who have needs, may be in a major crisis, or may just need a little encouragement. Taking the time to experience—or at least consider—someone else's situation can often help us overcome our own. Perhaps all that's needed is a visit to someone in the hospital, a meal prepared for someone who's just had surgery, an offer to babysit, or a simple invitation to go out for coffee. Offering our time and a listening ear can make a significant difference in someone's life.

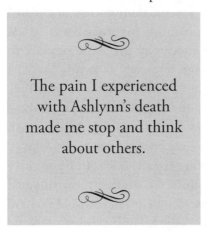

The pain I experienced with Ashlynn's death made me stop and think about others.

Aligning Priorities

God may use difficult circumstances to help us adjust our focus. Recently I watched my neighbor's house burn to the ground. The fire was the most consuming, powerful, and aggressive thing I've ever seen. I awoke to sights and sounds that can best be described as evil. The rushing roar, the bright lights, and the overwhelming heat seemed like a nightmare. We were helpless. All we could do was sit and watch while we waited for the fire department to respond. Thankfully, everyone escaped from the home; however, two other houses caught fire as the wind blew the embers. Our sense of security was challenged.

After the fire, I reflected on what I'd done earlier that day and made a mental note of the worries that had filled my mind. *What color will I paint my foyer? Will I be ready for our visitors who are coming in two days? Am I ever going to finish the laundry?* Suddenly, all of these things were insignificant. I had elevated them to a place of value and invested time and energy that I'll never regain. I questioned how often I wasted energy on trivial things.

Unfortunately, it often takes something tragic or life-altering to get our attention and help us adjust our focus. Immediately following the fire, everyone was just thankful that their families were alive; however, as time passed and the busyness of life crept in, I found myself returning to natural tendencies and thoughts. To maintain a level of joy, it's important to stay connected to the source, and that means making our relationship with God a priority. The better we know Him, the easier it is to seek His perspective in troubling times.

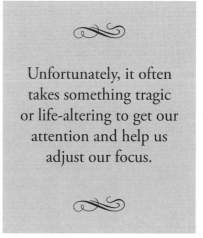

Unfortunately, it often takes something tragic or life-altering to get our attention and help us adjust our focus.

And remember, praise Him for what He has done and is doing in your life. Then wait with anticipation. He is friend and Father, so you don't have to endure hard times alone. Ask God to give you new eyes and a new perspective. Staying focused on bad circumstances makes matters worse.

The problem becomes all consuming, draining you physically and emotionally, leading you into hopelessness. A change in perspective—even the slightest change in your thinking—can make all the difference and may even allow you to embrace whatever hardship you face.

Longing for Heaven

My six-year-old daughter once said, "I wish life were like heaven." I realized she already knew too much about the hardships of this world. Her sister had died eight months earlier and she desperately wanted to hold and love her baby sister as she continued to grieve. Like me, she wondered what Ashlynn would be doing right now if she were still here. Unfortunately, her knowledge of painful circumstances doesn't stop there. She has seen the result of divorce in the lives of her cousins, and she wonders why families split apart. She has watched her grandmother battle cancer, and she wonders about illness. She has seen parents yell at their children in public, and she wonders what they possibly could have done to deserve such treatment. She has seen her friend's house burn to the ground, and she wonders if her home is safe. She understands the fragility of life and the finality of death.

Although still in kindergarten, my daughter's words remind me of an important perspective. She looks forward to heaven. It breaks my heart that she has experienced such pain and hardship at such a young age, but I feel a sense of comfort that she knows there's something far greater to look forward to. Heaven is our real home, so as Christians, shouldn't we all be longing for it? Shouldn't we all feel a little strange in this world, like it's not a perfect fit?

I'm not suggesting that we sit around and lament that we're stuck in this world. We should live life with passion and zeal, but we need to carefully choose how we invest our time and resources. We must focus on things with eternal value.

During the fire in our neighborhood, I became keenly aware of how quickly earthly treasures can be destroyed. I was reminded of what is really important and was thankful for my salvation and the safety of my family. Many of the thoughts and plans I'd had earlier in the day no longer had meaning. Material things can be replaced, but people and relationships cannot. So then why do we spend so much time trying to accumulate wealth and possessions, often at the expense of our families, friends, and loved ones? How often do we miss opportunities to spend quality time with our family? How often do we say an unkind word to our spouse or become impatient with our children because we're tired from the busyness of life?

God's greatest command is to love Him with our all heart, soul, and strength (Luke 10:27). If we work toward this goal, we'll be busy loving others instead of loving our possessions, our wealth, or our status. God wants us to be good stewards of what He's given us; however, we need to keep a healthy perspective. Our belongings cannot be taken with us when we die, and they won't bring ultimate happiness while we're here. Our time would be better spent storing up riches in heaven.

How do I make eternity my focus and still live a productive life on earth? The answer lies in having a close relationship with God. As we read God's word, pray, seek His will, and draw near to Him, He will guide us. Although He sometimes just wants us to be still in His presence, He'll also show us how we can be involved in His work right where we are, in the midst of everyday life.

And what a thrill it is to be used by God! The more we allow the Spirit to guide our thoughts and actions, the more fruitful we'll be. The more we demonstrate God's love, the more others will want what we have. Loving God with all our being not only transforms us; it makes a positive impact on those around us.

Just imagine if our families, communities, states, and nations turned to God. If everyone started living in a way that honored God, this life would feel a lot more like heaven and we'd be closer to home. So, I'll continue to press on toward the goal. In the meantime, I, like my daughter, wish life were like heaven.

God Says:

- "Consider it pure joy, my brothers, whenever you face trials of many kinds, because you know that the testing of your faith develops perseverance. Perseverance must finish its work so that you may be mature and complete, not lacking anything" (James 1:2–4).
- "Blessed is the man who perseveres under trial, because when he has stood the test, he will receive the crown of life that God has promised to those who love him" (James 1:12).
- "But rejoice that you participate in the sufferings of Christ, so that you may be overjoyed when his glory is revealed" (1 Pet. 4:13).
- "No, dear brothers and sisters, I have not achieved it, but I focus on this one thing: Forgetting the past and looking forward to what lies ahead, I press on to reach the end of the race and receive the heavenly prize for which God, through Christ Jesus, is calling us. . . . But we are citizens of heaven, where the Lord Jesus Christ lives. And we are eagerly waiting for him to return as our Savior. He will take our weak mortal bodies and change them into glorious bodies like his own, using the same power with which he will bring everything under his control" (Phil. 3:13–14; 20–21 NLT).
- "The mind of sinful man is death, but the mind controlled by the Spirit is life and peace" (Rom. 8:6).

- "And we know that God causes all things to work together for good to those who love God, to those who are called according to His purpose" (Rom. 8:28 NASB).
- "'For my thoughts are not your thoughts, neither are your ways my ways,' declares the LORD" (Isa. 55:8).

Your Chance to Dance:

- Dance in the rain. If you live in a particularly dry area, you're not off the hook. Instead, find a lawn sprinkler. It will achieve the same effect.
- Think about a past trial you have endured. Make a list of all the good things that resulted from it. What did you learn or how did you grow? How was God glorified? If you can't think of a personal trial that resulted in good, look for examples in the Bible, such as the stories about Joseph, Job, Ruth, or Paul.
- Think about others around you who may be suffering. Maybe there is an elderly shut-in, a person with a terminally ill child, someone going through divorce, or someone grieving the loss of a loved one who could use your company. Find a tangible way to reach out to them. If you're not able to help, at least call or send a note of encouragement.
- Make a list of other sufferers for whom you can pray. Start praying for them today.

Chapter Three

OUT OF CONTROL
AND INTO THE
ARMS OF GOD

Shortly after Ashlynn died, I morphed into a creature that was unrecognizable. As I would replay the days' events through my head, it was as if I was watching someone else. I couldn't make sense of my thoughts, let alone my behavior. In hindsight, I affectionately refer to that time as my "protective mommy mode." I had an intense need to protect my other two daughters. I had just experienced the most helpless feeling in the world—watching my child die and knowing that there was absolutely nothing I could do for her. I was at God's mercy. I had no control, so with every ounce of strength I could muster, I tried to gain a sense of control. God would reveal that I needed to turn things over to Him because, after all, the idea that I am in control is just an illusion.

Do you like to be in control of your life? I do. At least I like to feel as if I'm in control. I always have a plan . . . and Plan B . . . and Plan C . . . and Plan D. All of those alternate plans should probably be a clear indication that I'm not really in control, but I get them lined up anyway.

Why do we feel the need to be in control? Do we have a strong need for order? Is it a sense of security? Do we feel that we must be doing something in order to be productive?

Whatever the case, I've come to the realization that I have very little control over many of my circumstances. That's not to say that I'm a pawn that is passively moved from place to place. I simply understand that often the only thing I really control is how I react to things around me. I can't change how others treat me or what they think of me. I can't change how my family thinks or acts. I can only control my own thoughts, attitudes, and behavior.

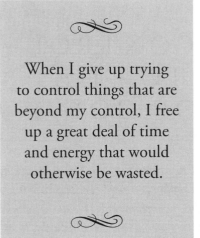

When I give up trying to control things that are beyond my control, I free up a great deal of time and energy that would otherwise be wasted.

As uncomfortable as my realization of my lack of control might be, I'm comforted greatly with the knowledge that God is in control. When I give up trying to control things that are beyond my control, I free up a great deal of time and energy that would otherwise be wasted. This allows me the opportunity for peace of mind, better sleep, and for investment of my efforts where I can actually have an impact.

Know Who God Really Is

It's easier to fall into the arms of someone you know and trust than into those of a stranger; therefore, it is imperative to know who God really is if you're going to fall back on Him—i.e. give up control and trust Him. He is creator, author, almighty, alpha and omega, loving, counselor, wonderful, and He wants a personal relationship with you. But don't just take my word for it. If you don't already know Him with confidence, start seeking Him. He has revealed Himself to us in the Bible, which is His Word to us. The Bible is God's primary way of letting us know about Himself. Some may believe the Bible is just a nice history book full of stories from the past, but it's actually His living Word—alive and active (Heb. 4:12). God speaks to all aspects of our lives through His Word if we're willing to listen.

Although I'd always known God as the Creator and I believed He loved me, it wasn't until recent years that I really developed a personal relationship with Him. Prior to that, I said prayers of thanksgiving and I called on Him during times of stress or trouble, but I didn't really know Him. My prayers seemed to vanish into thin air, and I hoped that at some later time I'd be able to look back and see if He'd answered them. I didn't truly know the depths of His love or the power of His Spirit. I was missing out.

You see, I knew about God, but I didn't know Him personally. It was sort of like being a part of a fan club. I knew God existed. I would listen as others said good stuff about Him and figured I knew Him too, when actually, all I had was their secondhand information. I did not enter into a personal relationship until God and I met together. He already knew me; I had to get to know Him.

If you don't feel that you really know God, I encourage you to begin a journey getting to know Him. Open your Bible and begin reading His Word. It is a revelation of Himself. Get to know Him. He's ready and waiting for you. I promise you won't be disappointed.

The Creator and His Master Plan

When bad things happen, it's hard to think that God is in control. How could a loving God possibly allow horrific things to happen? After September 11, 2001, many people questioned God. Our country reels in the aftermath of inexplicable tragedies like the Virginia Tech massacre and the Columbine shootings.

When bad things happen, we want answers. We ask, "Why did that happen? Who is to blame? Why didn't God stop it from happening? What will happen next? Does God really love me?" We will likely never find answers to these questions that totally satisfy us. But one thing is for sure, God is always in control. He may not have caused the trauma, but He knew about it long before it happened. Even with atrocities in life, rest assured that God will use it to bring glory to Himself and to advance His kingdom. Satan won't get the final word.

Shortly after I learned of Ashlynn's condition, the verse "Be still, and know that I am God" (Ps. 46:10) came to me from several different sources over the course of a few days. Someone wrote it in a card to me, it appeared in a booklet that someone shared with me, and I read it in one of my daily readings. It was clear to me that God was speaking. His words are quite emphatic and powerful. He is God, and I needed to be still and let that penetrate every fiber of my being. He was still in control even though my life was spinning wildly out of control. I wouldn't accomplish anything by worrying, and there wasn't anything I could do to change my situation. My only real option was to trust God. Anything other than prayer would have been a waste of time.

I had to trust that God had a greater plan.

I had to trust that God had a greater plan. I may not like His plan nor have chosen it for myself, but I had to make a choice: get with the program—His program—or whine and complain and expend every bit of my energy throwing a temper tantrum and a pity party. God would have allowed either choice. Ashlynn's death would still have occurred no matter how I reacted, but my journey would have been quite different. I had to trust that Ashlynn was fearfully and wonderfully made and that God had a plan and purpose for her life. She accomplished that purpose in two-and-a-half short days, and she was just as important to God as the rest of His children. I may never see all of the effects of her life, but I am certainly changed, and perhaps God will use me in some small way to reach others.

Are you struggling to trust God's plan? Are you questioning His sovereign right to use you or your child for His purposes? He can use anyone He chooses and any event or hardship for His good. And I do mean anything. The prophet Jeremiah helps us understand this truth when he says, "Ah, Sovereign LORD, you have made the heavens and the earth by your great power and outstretched arm. Nothing is too hard for you" (Jer. 32:17).

Without going into a lengthy discussion, I at least want to acknowledge the concept of free will. God created us to be thinking, reasoning beings, and He allows us to make choices. Yet, somehow He's still in control. God is aware of the choices we'll make even before we make them, and knows every detail of our current situation. We may or may not have created the mess around us. We make decisions that lead us down a certain path, but wherever we are, God can rescue us in His perfect timing and good can emerge if we give it over to Him.

Submit to God's Plan

My oldest daughter has always loved pretend play. She'll pretend to be the teacher, the mom, the baby, the dance instructor, or even the dog. One day when she was a preschooler, she looked at me and said, "Mom, you be Jesus and I'll be God." I was tempted to try to trade assignments with her. Of course I had to chuckle at her creativity and also wonder a bit about just how she might "play" God. But I also had to laugh because it

DANCING IN THE RAIN

amazes me how often God speaks to me through my children. How often had I wanted to be God—to be in charge, to hold the ultimate power, and have everyone else submit to me?

Ah, there's the "s" word with which we struggle—submit. It means "to yield to governance or authority."[1] I'm not sure which is the hardest part to digest, the fact that I have to yield, or the fact that someone else is in authority. Both parts of the definition mean giving in or giving up our rights, and in our "me first" society, this is counterintuitive and makes us quite uncomfortable. We like to do things our way, so submission can be hard to swallow.

The reality is, however, that God is our authority, the one to whom we must submit, and He's given us guidelines for our protection. Consider the Ten Commandments. He doesn't tell us not to commit adultery because He wants to ruin our fun. He gives this boundary because He knows what cheating can do to a marriage. Adultery has lifelong, detrimental effects, destroying trust, respect, and love, not to mention ripping the family apart. Even if husband and wife can forgive and preserve the marriage, scars remain in the family unit that can be passed down for generations. So God is trying to protect us from devastation, not to give harsh rules for the sake of exerting His power.

Submission is an act of love and respect. Submitting to God is in our best interest. He wants what is best for us, but He's not going to make us choose Him and His ways. Sadly, we won't know the fullness of His blessing if we don't.

Think about one of your childhood dreams. Perhaps you wanted to get married, have lots of children, and a great house with a picket fence. Perhaps you looked forward to having the perfect job. Maybe you just wanted to grow to be tall enough to ride the roller coasters at the nearby amusement park. Whatever the case, think about what happened as you began to accomplish those goals and dreams. Were you completely satisfied or was something still lacking? I think we are all secretly longing for more because whatever we thought would bring us satisfaction is somehow lacking. Jesus is the only solution to fill the void. He's the perfect size and fit for whatever empty place lurks deep within us.

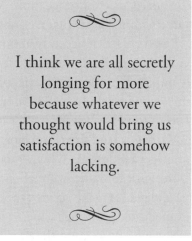

> I think we are all secretly longing for more because whatever we thought would bring us satisfaction is somehow lacking.

Complete satisfaction involves being satisfied in Christ, and being satisfied in Christ means submitting to His plan for our lives. His plans need to become our dreams and longings. First Corinthians 2:9 states, "No eye has seen, no ear has heard, no mind has conceived what God has prepared for those who love him". Although this is a reference to our eternal lives in heaven, I believe God can wow us during our earthly lives as well. The times when I've been in greatest awe have been times when God has revealed Himself to me, not when I've accomplished some earthly task or received a gift or treasure.

When we truly submit our hearts and lives to God, He becomes the driving force behind our desires and dreams. We're much more likely to see the realization of our dreams and feel a true sense of satisfaction when God is orchestrating it all. As Beth Moore says in her study, *Breaking Free*, "An unhappy woman usually needs a change of heart more than a change of circumstances."[2] Letting God be our true heart's desire changes how we feel about our circumstances.

Waiting on the Lord

Waiting on the Lord requires great discipline. God's time frame is not the same as ours. What seems like an eternity to us is perhaps a split second to God. It's so difficult for us to wait because we live in a fast-paced society in which we expect everything now. Faxes, e-mails, and instant messages have increased the speed of communication. We face a constant barrage of information about what we "need" to be doing.

I read an article recently about the lost art of doing nothing. Gone are the days of sitting on the back porch, sipping tea or lemonade while watching the sunset, talking to a child, or reading a good book. In fact, even our vacations are action-packed. I seem to need a vacation after returning from a vacation.

We have a hard time just being still. When forced to be still, we often get a little testy. Whether the drive-thru is taking too long or we're stuck in traffic, we're often appalled if we have to wait. We have digital cameras so we can immediately see our photos and immediately print them. We no longer wait for development.

Since we're so conditioned to having everything happen in an instant, what do we do when we pray and we don't get an immediate answer? Do we think God just doesn't care? Do we think that somehow God isn't interested or He's too busy? Do we begin to doubt God and His abilities? Perhaps we just stop waiting, make our own best guess at what should happen, and go ahead with our plans without Him.

In the Bible, there are many examples of people who had to wait. Think back to the story of Lazarus. Jesus knew that Lazarus was sick but didn't go to him. Lazarus had been dead for four days before Jesus arrived and brought him back to life. Can you imagine the grief and agony of Lazarus' family? I wonder what they did while they waited for Jesus.

Waiting was involved after Jesus' death as well. He did not rise until the third day. And He did not send the Holy Spirit until fifty days later.

So why does God make us wait? Perhaps it's to develop patience and character. Perhaps it's a test. Sometimes God wants us on our knees in prayer and surrender, and the quicker we get there, the quicker He'll relieve the pain. The reasons could be many and we may never know or understand; therefore, what we do while we're waiting is more important than why we have to wait.

Waiting on the Lord is not a passive activity. There's plenty to do while we're waiting for God's response. We should be praying while we wait. We should be praising Him while we wait. We should be examining our hearts and minds while we wait. Not only will we reap benefits from engaging in such activities, but the waiting itself will be more bearable. David conveys his confidence in the Lord when he says, "In the morning, O LORD, you hear my voice; in the morning I lay my requests before you and wait in expectation" (Ps. 5:3). It's this confidence that relieves our need to be in control and allows us to fully trust God.

Waiting on the Lord is not a passive activity.

No matter where we are in life, in God's arms is the best place to be. Whether we're just getting to know Him or we already have a great relationship, looking to Him frees us from needing to worry and stress about our circumstances.

Allow Him to be in control. He won't lead you astray.

God Says:

- "O Sovereign LORD, you are God! Your words are trustworthy, and you have promised these good things to your servant" (2 Sam. 7:28).
- "But as for me, it is good to be near God. I have made the Sovereign LORD my refuge; I will tell of all your deeds" (Ps. 73:28).

- "O Sovereign LORD, my strong deliverer, who shields my head in the day of battle" (Ps. 140:7).
- "O Sovereign LORD, you have begun to show to your servant your greatness and your strong hand. For what god is there in heaven or on earth who can do the deeds and mighty works you do?" (Deut. 3:24).
- "For You have been a defense for the helpless, a defense for the needy in his distress, a refuge from the storm, a shade from the heat" (Isa. 25:4 NASB).
- "Praise be to the God and Father of our Lord Jesus Christ, the Father of compassion and the God of all comfort" (2 Cor. 1:3).
- "Ah, Sovereign LORD, you have made the heavens and the earth by your great power and outstretched arm. Nothing is too hard for you" (Jer. 32:17).
- "Trust in the LORD with all your heart and lean not on your own understanding; in all your ways acknowledge him, and he will make your paths straight" (Prov. 3:5–6).
- "'For I know the plans I have for you,' declares the LORD, 'plans to prosper you and not to harm you, plans to give you hope and a future'" (Jer. 29:11).
- "In the morning, O LORD, you hear my voice; in the morning I lay my requests before you and wait in expectation" (Ps. 5:3).
- "He will make your righteousness shine like the dawn, the justice of your cause like the noonday sun. Be still before the LORD and wait patiently for him; do not fret when men succeed in their ways, when they carry out their wicked schemes" (Ps. 37:6–7).
- "I am still confident of this: I will see the goodness of the LORD in the land of the living. Wait for the LORD; be strong and take heart and wait for the LORD" (Ps. 27:13–14).

- "Brothers, as an example of patience in the face of suffering, take the prophets who spoke in the name of the Lord. As you know, we consider blessed those who have persevered. You have heard of Job's perseverance and have seen what the Lord finally brought about. The Lord is full of compassion and mercy" (James 5:10–11).

Your Chance to Dance:

- Choose a day to practice letting God be in total control of your schedule. Begin the day with prayer, offering yourself to God. Let Him guide your day.
- If you are tempted to worry about something, find Scripture verses that remind you of God's sovereignty and control. Write them on note cards and review them frequently.
- Make a list of the names of God. Review the list regularly to remind yourself how big God really is. Here's a start:[2]

Elohim—All powerful, Creator
El Elyon—God Most High
El Roi—The God who sees and watches over you
El Shaddai—The All-Sufficient One, "God Almighty"
Adonai—Lord, Master, Ruler
Jehovah or Yahweh—The personal name of God, "Lord"
Jehovah-Jireh—The Lord who will provide
Jehovah-Rophe—The Lord who heals
Jehovah-Nissi—The Lord our banner, "Victory is ours"
Jehovah-Mekoddishkem—The Lord that sanctifies you, "Makes you holy"
Jehovah-Shalom—The Lord is our peace
Jehovah-Shammah—The Lord who is there
Jehovah-Tsidkenu—The Lord our righteousness

Chapter Four

GOD'S ENDLESS LOVE

*T*he moment Ashlynn was born, there was a flurry of activity in the operating room. She was being examined. I was being stitched up from the C-section. Someone raced down the hall to get my mother so she could hold Ashlynn, then hurry to get my other two daughters. Family and friends were anxiously awaiting the fate of the delivery. The anesthesiologist exited to go handle his next assignment. Our pastor, who recognized the anesthesiologist from when I was whisked to surgery a few minutes earlier, reached out and grabbed him. "Is the baby alive?" he questioned intently.

As the doctor answered yes, cheers erupted in the room. They were cheering for my daughter who was imperfect in so many ways. She didn't meet societal standards, yet they didn't care. They loved her and saw her for the special gift of life that she was. The thought of it still brings tears.

God Created Us

We were created to worship God, to bring God glory, and to walk in companionship with Him. Genesis 1:26 tells us that God created man in His own image. God saw all that He had made and He declared it all as very good. He was pleased with His entire creation, but especially with man and woman. Psalm 139 tells us that we are wonderfully made. "For you created my inmost being; you knit me together in my mother's womb" (Ps. 139:13). Even after the fall of man and the downward spiral of humanity that scarred the beauty of what God had created, God saved Noah and his family so they could repopulate the earth. And He took it a step further—He promised never to destroy the world again by flood. God gave man a second chance because of His love for us.

Before the creation of the earth, God already had a legion of angels to praise and worship Him, yet He created us anyway. Not only that, He also gave us dominion over the earth. And although His desire is that we love Him and choose Him, He has given us free will, the absolute freedom to make choices and decisions on our own.

God Is Real and Relevant

Five weeks after Ashlynn died, I was scheduled to go to a Christian women's conference. At the last minute I tried to back out, but my husband insisted that I go. At a time when I had been questioning God's love for me, I trudged on to this conference having no idea what the topic would be. I only knew that Beth Moore was the speaker. As I understand, she doesn't publicize the topic in advance because she follows God's leading on what to present and often doesn't know herself until a few weeks before the conference.

So I arrived at the conference and discovered that the focus would be God's immeasurable love for us. How ironic. Or was it? It was exactly what I needed at that moment, and God knew it. She shared in detail how God is very specific about various measurements throughout the Bible; yet He tells us that His love for us has no limits. His love is so great that it cannot be contained or defined by measurements; it's immeasurable. The Bible mentions His unfailing love thirty-two times and the fact that His love endures forever forty-four times. Additionally, Psalm 108:4 states, "For great is your love, higher than the heavens; your faithfulness reaches to the skies."

During one of the breaks, I stayed in the arena to pray. As I sat in my seat, my face in my hands, I poured out my heart to God. I was sobbing. I had been distant from God the previous several weeks and was really struggling. As I cried, I told God that I needed to feel His presence in a very real way. I needed to feel His comfort and wanted to feel His arms around me. Within seconds, a woman approached me, wrapped her arms around me, and began to pray. As she hugged me and prayed, she knew just what to say. She prayed about how God chose me and loved me. I'm convinced she was from God—maybe not an angel, but someone who was obedient to the Holy Spirit's leading to come over to me. I have no idea who she was, and she disappeared as quickly as she had appeared.

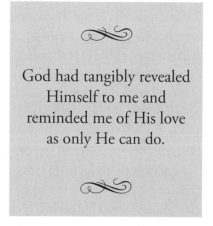

God had tangibly revealed Himself to me and reminded me of His love as only He can do.

I was speechless. God had tangibly revealed Himself to me and reminded me of His love as only He can do. Tears still pool in my eyes whenever I think of that moment. God met me where I was and showed His love just as I asked. Perhaps He had just been waiting for me to ask.

God wants to be real to each of us, not just a passing thought or "magic genie" we call on in times of need. He will reveal Himself to us in real and mighty ways when we ask Him and make time for Him.

God Loves Us in Spite of Our Imperfections

I was reminded at that conference that as much as I loved Ashlynn, God loved me more. How hard that was to imagine! I loved Ashlynn in spite of her imperfections and weaknesses. Ashlynn's hands were twisted, her feet deformed, and she had a heart and brain that weren't able to sustain life. Yet, that's not what I saw when I looked at her. I loved her more than I'm humanly able to convey. And my love for her lives on. Her life has come to represent many special things to me.

Through Ashlynn's life, God revealed that He feels the same way about me. He loves me in spite of my imperfections and inabilities. He knows that I can't sustain life without Him. He knows that my life is but a breath, yet He loves me still. His love for me has never changed and never will.

God feels the same about you. We don't have to earn His love; it's free and unconditional. I've struggled with this concept for much of my life. I often waver between feeling like I've disappointed God and feeling like I need to be doing more to please Him. The reality is that He loves me even when I make poor choices. There's nothing I can do to make Him love me any more. He already loves me as much as He ever could, and He demonstrated that at the cross.

After experiencing the death of my child, I realize how much God must have loved us to have given up His Son. I didn't give Ashlynn up willingly, yet God chose to be separated from His Son as Jesus took on the sin of the world. What a demonstration of love for us—His fallen, sinful creation. He wanted to break the barrier between us and Him and restore our relationship, and Jesus was willing to pay the price and be the ultimate sacrifice. I struggle to comprehend that kind of love.

God Gives Good Things

"If you, then, though you are evil, know how to give good gifts to your children, how much more will your Father in heaven give good gifts to those who ask him!" (Matt. 7:11). Our heavenly Father is superior to any human parent we can imagine, and He loves us more than the most doting mothers and fathers. Let's look at some of the good things God promises us.

In Ephesians, chapter one, we're told of several spiritual blessings. We are blessed, chosen, adopted, redeemed, and forgiven, not because we deserve it, but because of our faith in Jesus Christ. Along with salvation, other passages of Scripture promise us that we'll be co-heirs with Christ (Rom. 8:17), and we'll have a heavenly inheritance (John 14:2, 1 Pet. 1:3–4).

God extends His amazing grace and mercy over and over again. As a child, I learned that grace is an acronym for "God's riches at

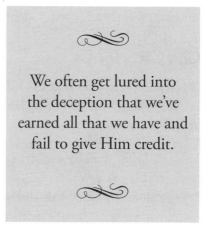

We often get lured into the deception that we've earned all that we have and fail to give Him credit.

Christ's expense." I have also often heard that grace is receiving things we don't deserve, while mercy is *not* receiving what we do deserve. I praise God that He loves us enough to be both gracious and merciful.

He also provides for our earthly needs. "Every good and perfect gift is from above, coming down from the Father of the heavenly lights" (James 1:17). However, we often get lured into the deception that we've earned all that we have and fail to give Him credit. As we take a mental inventory of all that we have and look through the eyes of thankfulness, we begin to realize how much God actually provides and dotes on us.

In all of His goodness, it's important to remember that God promises to give us what we need. It doesn't mean we always get what we want. My young daughters would each love to have a TV in their bedroom. However, I don't feel that's in their best interest. It would decrease the amount of time they spend interacting with each other and the family and would increase their exposure to advertising and other pressures from the outside world. There's also research to show that having a TV in the bedroom is detrimental for health, leading to poor habits such as overeating and a sedentary lifestyle.[1] Because we love our daughters, we won't grant their request. Likewise, God sometimes vetoes our requests because He knows what's best.

God Cares for Us

It's clear in Scripture that God cares for us and He's interested in every part of our lives. God knows everything about us. Look at Psalm 139, verses 1–10:

> O LORD, you have searched me
> and you know me.
> You know when I sit and when I rise;
> you perceive my thoughts from afar.
> You discern my going out and my lying down;
> you are familiar with all my ways.
> Before a word is on my tongue
> you know it completely, O LORD.
> You hem me in—behind and before;
> you have laid your hand upon me.
> Such knowledge is too wonderful for me,
> too lofty for me to attain.
> Where can I go from your Spirit?
> Where can I flee from your presence?
> If I go up to the heavens, you are there;
> if I make my bed in the depths, you are there.

If I rise on the wings of the dawn,
if I settle on the far side of the sea,
even there your hand will guide me,
your right hand will hold me fast.

God is concerned with every detail of our lives. Nothing is too small or too big for Him. He loves us so much that He attends to every thought and action.

My grandmother was having a rough day and had misplaced her dentures. She desperately needed them and became more and more frustrated as she searched her entire house for them to no avail. Finally in exasperation, she sat down in her chair and pleaded for God's help. As she finished praying, a sense of peace came over her. Arising from her chair, she walked to the kitchen and over to the stove to open the drawer below the oven where she stored her pans. There in the drawer lay her teeth. To this day, she laughs about this but also thanks God for being interested in every detail of her life.

Another example of God being concerned about the details involves my oldest daughter when she was just three years old. After riding in the back seat for quite some time with her inconsolable, crying baby sister, she began to pray aloud, "Dear God, please make my sister stop crying." Instantly, there was silence in the car. A glance in the rearview mirror gave me a glimpse of my daughter smiling with delight

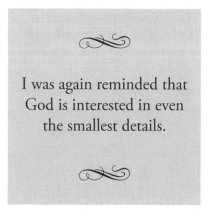

I was again reminded that God is interested in even the smallest details.

because God had answered her prayer. I was again reminded that God is interested in even the smallest details. Both my daughter and I learned a little more about trusting God in that small moment, and I took great pleasure in praising God for the lesson.

I'll share one final example. One of my friends recalls having a list of things she prayed about as a child. She prayed that she'd get to see a real hot air balloon, travel to New York, own a computer, and marry a man who would like plain cheeseburgers and plain pizza. The first three requests were granted fairly quickly in various, unexpected ways. The husband obviously came much later, but he indeed had the specific eating preferences she requested. The simple prayers of a child broke through to heaven and God replied with a "yes" to all of them. I laugh when I think of it, and her husband loves to tell people that it's her fault that he has peculiar tastes. He also warns never to invite her to join a pool with you when purchasing a lottery ticket, because as a child she also prayed Proverbs 30:8b–9, which says, "Give me neither poverty nor riches, but give me only my daily bread. Otherwise, I may have too much and disown you and say, 'Who is the LORD?' Or I may become poor and steal, and so dishonor the name of my God."

On the opposite end of the spectrum, God is concerned with the "big stuff" in our lives too. He cares about the mess we're in or the big decisions we face related to finances, relationships, careers, etc. He cares about every detail of our lives.

Although God doesn't always answer every prayer quickly and with a "yes," we can still trust that He cares. He wants to hear from us and tells us to cast our cares on Him. Psalm 55:22 states, "Cast your cares on the LORD and he will sustain you," and 1 Peter 5:7 instructs, "Cast all your anxiety on him because he cares for you." God is faithful and trustworthy; we can believe His word. He affirms His love for us repeatedly and reminds us at least ten times in the Bible that He'll never forsake us.

So, we have reason to be joyful because of God's love. No matter the circumstances—even the devastating death of a child—we can be confident that God still loves us. He has a track record of being involved in the details, no matter how big or small. When we turn to Him, He will reveal His presence and comfort, even in the midst of trials.

God Says:

- "How great is the love the Father has lavished on us, that we should be called children of God!" (1 John 3:1).
- "For as high as the heavens are above the earth, so great is his love for those who fear him" (Ps. 103:11).
- "And I pray that you, being rooted and established in love, may have power, together with all the saints, to grasp how wide and long and high and deep is the love of Christ, and to know this love that surpasses knowledge—that you may be filled to the measure of all the fullness of God" (Eph. 3:17–19).
- "See, I have engraved you on the palms of my hands" (Isa. 49:16).
- "Your love, O LORD, reaches to the heavens, your faithfulness to the skies" (Ps. 36:5).
- "'Though the mountains be shaken and the hills be removed, yet my unfailing love for you will not be shaken nor my covenant of peace be removed,' says the LORD, who has compassion on you" (Isa. 54:10).
- "But you are a forgiving God, gracious and compassionate, slow to anger and abounding in love" (Neh. 9:17).
- "O Israel, put your hope in the LORD, for with the LORD is unfailing love and with him is full redemption" (Ps. 130:7).
- "Give thanks to the God of gods. His love endures forever" (Ps. 136:2).
- "For God so loved the world that he gave his one and only Son, that whoever believes in him shall not perish but have eternal life" (John 3:16).

- "God demonstrates His own love toward us, in that while we were still sinners, Christ died for us. Much more then, having now been justified by His blood, we shall be saved from wrath through Him. For if when we were enemies we were reconciled to God through the death of His Son, much more, having been reconciled, we shall be saved by His life" (Rom. 5:8–10 NKJV).

Your Chance to Dance:

- Find a small cross that you can carry with you as a reminder of God's love for you. Keep it in a coat pocket, in your purse, or in your car.
- Start a "God's Presence Today" journal. At the end of every day, write down ways you observed God's presence that day. Maybe you saw Him in a beautiful sunset or in protection from some type of danger. You may have experienced God's presence through healing from an illness or a special revelation of His Word spoken to you. On days you're tempted to question His love, pull out your journal and review the lists you've made.

Chapter Five

YOUR RELATIONSHIP
WITH GOD

We were blessed to have a photographer take pictures of Ashlynn the day she was born. The photographer even compiled them into a beautiful slide show to include at Ashlynn's memorial service. For many weeks after Ashlynn's death, those treasured pictures comforted me daily. Then one day, I realized I hadn't watched the slide show for about a week. What was happening? Was I forgetting about her? Was I a terrible mother? As I thought about it, I realized that although I cherished the photographs we had, they weren't the real thing. They weren't the living and breathing Ashlynn. I'm very thankful to have the pictures, and the pictures stimulate warm memories, but there is no substitute for her actual presence. The fact remains that she'll always be missing from our earthly family.

We often get caught up with religion and lose sight of our relationship with God. The two are not synonymous. "A religion is a set of common beliefs and practices generally held by a group of people, often codified as prayer, ritual, and religious law."[1] Notice the structural nature of religion involving rituals and laws. By contrast, a relationship is a personal connection between two people. Just as my pictures of Ashlynn are no substitute for her actual presence, so the practice of a religion is no substitute for having a relationship with God.

Our relationship with our Creator should be anything but a set of codes and practices. Our relationship with God should be personal and real. Christ died so we'd have direct access to the Almighty. Moreover, the Holy Spirit was sent as a gift to believers so we can have a personal relationship with God. Our relationship with Him is the most important factor of dealing with any hardship. During trying times, I have found seven key components that help our relationship with God grow closer: honesty with God, trust in God, humility before God, faith in God, prayer, listening to God, and turning from worldly wisdom.

Our relationship with God should be personal and real.

Honesty with God

God already knows our hearts. He knows our every thought, action, and attitude. Adam and Eve tried to hide from God when they were in the midst of blatant sin. They covered themselves because they were ashamed and felt vulnerable as they were exposed. If we're honest with ourselves, we'll see that we're a lot like them. We try to put on a happy face and make our best impressions when we're out in the world.

I think back to countless Sunday mornings when our family was quite out of sorts as we were getting ready for church. As we pulled into the parking lot—or on a really bad day, as we walked through the sanctuary doors—we put on our we've-got-it-all-together faces. I'm not suggesting that we display all our troubles and issues for the world to see, but be careful not to take this habit into your relationship with God and find yourself hiding from Him. I also think we need to be willing to take risks in sharing with others in authentic ways.

Women battle an array of wars. We fight depression, anxiety, anger management, alcoholism, guilt from a past abortion, failed marriages, infertility, childhood sexual abuse, drug abuse, emotional abuse, food addiction, eating disorders, grief over a child with special needs, grief from the loss of a child or spouse, and the list goes on. Each of these issues are even represented by women active in church—seemingly happy women who appear to be living successful, fulfilling lives. Some women going through these problems may actually be happy and okay; however, many are putting on performances deserving of a standing ovation. It's hard work to ignore pain.

Honesty with God is the first step in finding comfort and healing. If we're willing to be honest with God, He's ready to hear our cries and begin restoration. In the Beatitudes, Jesus teaches that those who mourn will be comforted. He is specifically referring to mourning over our sins, which means being painfully honest with ourselves and with God.

Even though we know we're all sinners, we may not be able to see the sin in our own lives. If that's the case, we should pray for God's guidance in revealing that sin. Satan doesn't want us to recognize it. He wants us to rationalize it, cover it, make excuses for it, etc. He knows that sin is a wedge between us and God and he wants to keep us from getting too close to God. As we recognize and confess our sin, God forgives us and restores our relationship with Himself, thus thwarting Satan's plans for us.

What about when our pain is not a result of a sin? God still wants our honesty. He wants us to call out to Him so He can do more than just rescue us; He'll plant us on solid ground.

Psalm 40:2 says, "He lifted me out of the slimy pit, out of the mud and mire; he set my feet on a rock and gave me a firm place to stand." All that's necessary is that we believe His promises and trust in Him.

Trust in God

Trust is an interesting concept involving dependence on or a belief or confidence in someone or something. Sometimes trust is easy; sometimes it's not. Most of us never question whether the sun is going to rise the next morning. Based on our knowledge and experience, we trust it will. Perhaps we exhibit the same kind of trust in our car. Assuming we have a vehicle in good,

Fear keeps us from following God's plan for our lives.

working condition, we trust it will start and get us to our destination once we put the key in the ignition and shift it into gear. However, trust in relationships is much more challenging.

Fear is the opposite of trust. It is the enemy of trust. In our relationship with God, fear keeps us from following God's plan for our lives. Fear paralyzes us. Being unable to forge ahead in life's journey is an indication of a lack of trust in God.

A woman shared with me that she thought God was leading her to simplify her life and cut back on some of her many activities. She was feeling overwhelmed and empty. Although she longed for something to bring her satisfaction, she refused to follow God's leading to simplify so she could focus on Him and rely on Him to fill the emptiness inside. Instead, she chose two new part-time jobs that engulfed her time.

Was it outright defiance for her to go against what she thought God wanted her to do, or was she simply afraid to let go of what she could build for herself? Perhaps she was afraid that the opportunity to work wouldn't present itself again. Perhaps she was fearful that she hadn't really heard God correctly. Maybe, though, she was afraid to simplify because she'd have to abandon her own way of doing things and leap into God's outstretched, yet invisible arms. Whatever the case, I believe her actions demonstrated a lack of trust in God.

When my middle daughter was two, she experienced the laws of physics like never before. On a chilly March day with typical gusty winds and a light drizzle falling, she held her little umbrella over her head. As the next gust blew past, it got under that umbrella and my daughter became airborne—she was a true Mary Poppins. She traveled several yards before she landed again. Never did it occur to her to let go of the umbrella, so she went along for the ride. Eyes wide, she was defying gravity and living a new experience. After landing, we all laughed, but the ride seemed much more fun after knowing she was safely on the ground. There was fear in that brief moment of flight.

My daughter's anti-gravity experience and response made me think about how we interact with God during uncertain times. Do we hold onto Him as He leads us and embark upon the ride He has planned, or do we let go? If we let go, we may miss the ride of our lives. Although it may be frightening, trusting God—holding on to Him—will yield the greatest experiences we could ever imagine.

When Ashlynn died, I had to trust that God knew what He was doing and hadn't made some horrible mistake. I didn't feel it, so I had to trust that He really did love me, that He would heal my hurts and heal my oldest daughter's anxiety. I remember telling my grief counselor that I knew I was going to be OK, I just didn't like the process of getting there. God can use the discomfort in our lives to produce growth. I held on as God taught me to trust Him by pushing me out of my comfort zone. The growth I experienced during this process has enriched the relationship I have with Him. My life's not perfect, but I would never want to go back to the way things were.

God's Word says, "When you pass through the waters, I will be with you; and when you pass through the rivers, they will not sweep over you. When you walk through the fire, you will not be burned; the flames will not set you ablaze" (Isa. 43:2). Although there are many promises of God's love and protection in the Bible, after Ashlynn died I struggled to believe them. My head believed, but my heart wasn't on the same page. I was flooded with emotion. A wise friend reminded me to "believe it even when you don't feel it." She was essentially telling me that I needed to continue trusting and believing God's Word even if it didn't feel like truth. Eventually, my heart caught up and connected with my head. Why should I discount God's love for me simply because I was hurting and He didn't do things the way

Why should I discount God's love for me simply because I was hurting and He didn't do things the way I thought He should?

I thought He should? God never promised us freedom from painful circumstances, but He has faithfully and repeatedly shown His love for me. Slowly, I was able to overcome my doubts and believe again that His Word is absolute truth.

So, whatever your struggle or hurt, try to look for ways in which God may want you to trust Him. Maybe He wants you to step out and try something new. Or maybe He wants you to trust His timing and His ability to see you through the difficult time. I encourage you to step out in faith and soar with Him in that trust. Although scary, it will be worth the ride.

Humility Before God

Most of us feel about the word *humility* about the same as we feel about the word *submission*. We're not too fond of either of them. Yet, God detests pride (see Prov. 29:23, Isa. 2:11, 17), so we should take note and examine our lives in this area. God had been working on me to show me where pride needed to be stricken from my life. He started revealing to me some of the prideful thoughts and attitudes I held. It's never a particularly pleasant experience when God decides I need to work on an area in my life. He's very persistent with me, so I've learned that the quicker I "get it," the quicker He'll move on to something else. (Of course, moving on to something else isn't always so enjoyable either, but there's usually a break in between.)

As I've looked back at my journals, I can clearly see when God was trying to grow me in specific characteristics at various times because there are obvious themes in fairly short spaces of time.

The issue of pride continued to spring up. I didn't consider myself a prideful person, but God clearly saw the pride in my life. I had grown in my relationship with God over the course of a couple of years and I began to consider myself "more spiritual" than my husband. It wasn't a conscious thought, but it would leak out in conversations with him. At times, I would imply that I knew God's direction for our lives better than he did. Or I would subtly point out that I was more dedicated and faithful in prayer than he was. As God began to show me these prideful thoughts and attitudes, I was reminded that my relationship with God is unique and individual. I wasn't in a competition with my husband, or anyone else for that matter. I am just as much a sinner as my husband is and God loves each

63

of us equally. As I experienced these revelations I began to ask for forgiveness and prayed for strength to change my thoughts and attitudes.

I was feeling pretty good about the progress I was making in this area of pride—a sure sign that I still had work to do. On one particular Sunday morning, I became annoyed with my husband's behavior. I made some one-line comment to him about my irritation and then went on getting ready for church. In the car on our way to service, I was still aggravated and feeling a little righteous in my assessment of him. He dropped my daughter and me off at the children's wing so I could take her to her class. As I walked to the door, I suddenly felt something drop on my head. I was absolutely disgusted and mortified when I realized I had just been bombed by a bird. What a humbling experience to have bird poop in your hair. As I rushed to the bathroom to assess the damage, I realized God was trying to get my attention in His own creative and humorous way. Just as I had sent a zinger at my husband earlier that morning, God had sent His own zinger at me. I truly deserved it. As I stood in the bathroom and removed the bird's "present" from my hair, I began to pray, asking forgiveness for my pride, bad attitude, and poor behavior. I prayed for cleansing—in every sense of the word! I then laughed all the way to the worship service.

Interestingly enough, God spoke to me very clearly in the service that morning. I arrived at church in a foul mood, not ready to hear God, but He got my attention and I had a change of heart. I was open to Him and He spoke. Pretty amazing!

You better believe that I check the condition of my heart on Sunday mornings now before getting out of the car. I know that a lot can happen to the head and heart from the brief walk from the parking lot to the church doors. I would much rather arrive with a humble spirit than have God find a way to humble me.

Faith in God

"Now faith is being sure of what we hope for and certain of what we do not see" (Heb. 11:1). Although we're given this very clear definition of faith, it's often difficult to quantify our faith. We do know, however, that faith is a key component in our relationship with God. We are also told, "Without faith it is impossible to please God" (Heb. 11:6).

So how do we develop a deeper faith in God? Good question. We can start by moving close to Him. The closer we are to God, the easier faith becomes. As we come to know Him personally, our faith grows. God doesn't expect blind faith. He gives us His Word—the Bible—as a revelation of Himself. He offers Himself to us, but we share responsibility in getting to know Him.

This is similar to our human relationships. We don't often trust and believe complete strangers. The more we know about a person, the more comfortable we are with him or her. We can then form an assessment about whether or not we can have faith in that individual.

The Old Testament relates a story of a time of great drought and famine during Elijah's life. While others struggled during this hardship, God provided for Elijah by directing him to a brook in the ravine and by feeding him with food carried by the ravens. When the stream dried up, God instructed Elijah to go to the widow at Zarephath. This woman possessed only enough oil and flour to make one last meal for herself and her son; however, God commanded her to feed Elijah.

When Elijah arrived at the woman's house, she explained her lack to the prophet. Still, Elijah told her to prepare a small cake of bread for him and that her supplies would not run out. Out of obedience and faith, she did as she was instructed. Sure enough, her flour and oil did not run out and during the entire length of the famine she continued to have food.

Some time later, this same widow's son became ill and died; however, through prayer, Elijah brought him back to life. The widow responded, "Now I know that you are a man of God and that the word of the LORD from your mouth is the truth" (1 Kings 17:24).

It's interesting to me that the woman had already witnessed the miracle of her extended food supply, but it wasn't until her son was brought back to life that she said she believed Elijah was a man of God.

How often do we respond the same way? We may witness God's provisions or presence, yet our faith remains small. When faced with new trials, our spiritual knees buckle. If we would only just remember what God has done before. He is able to use the new trials as building blocks to a stronger faith, so eventually we come to know His true nature and fully trust Him.

God tells us that He's the perfecter of our faith (Heb. 12:2). Perhaps He allows trials and challenging circumstances to test us. He already knows our response, so we're not demonstrating our faith to Him. The tests reveal our faith to ourselves that we might learn and grow through them. The stronger our faith; the closer our relationship. Likewise, the closer our relationship; the stronger our faith. It's a lovely cycle, forming a circle of strength in which our faith is constantly nourished.

Prayer

Have you ever felt so bad, tired, overwhelmed, or lost that you couldn't even pray? I was there. After Ashlynn was born, my prayer life nearly ceased. I would thank God for bringing her into this world alive, but beyond that I didn't have much to say to Him. Perhaps I was numb. Perhaps I was shocked. Whatever it was that I was feeling, I know I didn't feel capable of praying. What could I possibly say to God? Worse yet was the burning question—did He even care? I knew in my core that more than ever I needed to be praying, yet I couldn't.

After several weeks of this, I began questioning why it was happening. I knew I needed to stay close to God more than ever, yet I couldn't muster the desire or strength to talk to Him. I missed the closeness I'd experienced with Him during my pregnancy. I had totally relied on Him and He had sustained me and given me strength. Now I was turning my back on Him.

I could verbalize the desire and the need I felt to be close to God, yet I couldn't seem to make myself draw near.

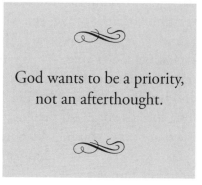

God wants to be a priority, not an afterthought.

Thankfully, I decided to confide in a friend about this struggle and I asked her to pray for me. I asked her to pray that God would ignite my desire to be with Him and communicate with Him. And praise God, He answered her prayer . . . quickly!

God wants to be a priority, not an afterthought. He enjoys constant communication with us. I used to think that prayer was a formal, structured activity and that I had to do it just right in order for it to work. How wrong I was! God just wants me to talk to Him, plain and simple. He doesn't require fancy words or for us to act more "spiritual" than we are. He just wants us to be honest and real.

Listening to God

Listening is an important part of communication and is essential to a healthy relationship, yet most of us aren't very good at it. When each of my daughters was three years old, they expressed very profound statements about listening.

"I'll be a good listener when I turn four," were the words that rolled off the tongue of my eldest daughter. Three years later, her younger sister equated hearing to listening and said, "I don't hear very well because I have little ears."

How often do we do this with God? Either we promise to be better listeners later when we have more time, or we claim to be lacking the necessary equipment to hear God's voice.

Hearing from God is one of the greatest joys in my life. I struggle to fathom that the Creator of the universe would take the time to speak to me; yet, when I make myself available to Him, He does so repeatedly. This never ceases to amaze and excite me. God's voice renews my spirit. During some of my most troubling times, His voice has broken through the chaos, and my connection with Him becomes my source for joy. I long for His voice and presence sustaining me and reminding me that He's in control and everything is going to be okay.

Let me clarify—I don't hear audible voices. God speaks to me primarily through His Word. At other times, He uses circumstances or people in my life to speak to me. I have even heard Him through the voices of my children and through my own voice. Many times I've said something to my children and God has made it clear that the words I just spoke to them applied to my relationship with Him.

Jesus tells us, "My sheep listen to my voice; I know them, and they follow me" (John 10:27). I didn't like this verse for a long time because I didn't feel like God spoke to me. I could see evidence of God around me through events, circumstances, and even nature; but I didn't hear anything directly from Him for myself. I didn't hear direction, guidance, encouragement, comfort, or even reprimand, so I started to question if I even belonged to Him. People would give their testimonies and share how God directed them, and I'd wonder how God spoke to them.

Eventually, through multiple Bible studies and godly leaders, I learned how to hear God's voice. It was no big mystery. Since I wasn't reading the Bible, I wasn't hearing from Him. How could I expect to hear His voice if I refused to expose myself to His words?

I had tried reading the Bible on many occasions but usually lost interest quickly, so I started praying that God would give me a desire to read His Word. It didn't happen in a day, but over time He answered that prayer. The more I studied, the more I was able to see the relevance of God's Word to my life. I became curious about what the Bible said about certain topics and would go on a search. I prayed that God's Word would come alive to me and that I'd have understanding when I read it. When I finally started reading the Bible, God started speaking to me. The more He spoke, the more I craved.

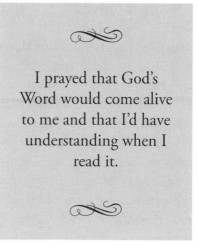

I prayed that God's Word would come alive to me and that I'd have understanding when I read it.

I truly believe this has been the key to my surviving the death of Ashlynn. My connection to God is my saving grace.

Turning from Worldly Wisdom

How often in life do we consult our friends about what we should do in a situation? Many times, our friends willingly share their opinions and advice with us because they care and they want to help. But who cares more about us? Even though I know I should go to God and His Word when confronted with difficult situations, I find that I often stop and think, "Who should I call?" Instead of calling God (i.e., praying and reading the Bible), I call my earthly friends. Instead of immediately taking my concern to the Creator of the universe, I call a buddy.

Why don't we think of God as our best friend? Although I slip back into old habits from time to time, as my relationship with God has grown, I find that I'm quicker to turn to Him for help. I know that I can take any decision or problem to Him and He will guide me. Though not always on my time frame, He always comes through. Matthew 7:8 says, "For everyone who asks receives; he who seeks finds; and to him who knocks, the door will be opened." Our heavenly Father knows best and gives us His best advice. What more could I ask when I need guidance?

He helped me learn of His ability to be there for me during my pregnancy with Ashlynn. The doctor was emphatic that Ashlynn would die, likely before even taking a breath in this world. Based on her scientific knowledge, the results of the amniocentesis, and her past experience, she was confident in her judgment. Many well-meaning people with whom we shared this diagnosis had their own ideas about what we should think, believe, do, etc. Each person shared his or her expertise with us as we were processing our emotions and assessing the circumstances.

At the other extreme was a Christian counselor who shared her beliefs about healing with us. She believed (and offered Scripture to support her opinion) that physical healing was always God's will and that it was up to us (my husband and me) to receive that healing for our baby. The majority of our friends and family members held beliefs that fell somewhere between that of the medical doctor and those of the counselor. Most would say they believed that God had the ability to heal Ashlynn if He so desired, but implied that we shouldn't get our hopes up because miracles don't really happen much these days. I struggled with what to believe, which ultimately led me closer to God in my search for truth.

As I wrestled with the possibility of healing, I began to think that I needed to have just the right people praying for us. I wanted those with "connections." This wasn't the time for ordinary prayers. I was desperate. I didn't believe that God valued my prayers. I felt there were other, more godly people that He'd rather hear. Perhaps, if those other, more godly people did the asking, I'd be more likely to get the answer I wanted. I was somehow putting value and trust in the prayers of other believers instead of my relationship with God.

> I struggled with what to believe, which ultimately led me closer to God in my search for truth.

Several people and organizations came to mind and I began to wonder about how I should approach them and what I should say. As I write, I chuckle at the plans I made. I was on a mission, strategizing and searching for those I deemed most qualified to do the praying and get God to hear and answer.

I'm almost certain God was laughing at me as He gently revealed His message to me the first time. "Stop trusting in man," he whispered as he had to Isaiah (Isa. 2:22). Oh! God reminded me that I have a direct line to Him myself, just like all other believers do. How amazing to know that He wanted me to personally trust and seek Him instead of relying on others.

I'm not suggesting that we shouldn't invite others to pray with us. It's always a good idea to pray with other believers; however, we should not neglect to first seek God ourselves and trust that He loves us and hears our prayers.

Living Out Your Relationship in Practice

As with any relationship, the more committed we are, the more we invest our time and ourselves. If the other party reciprocates, a close relationship usually follows. Imagine if you were always too busy for your friends or your husband or your children. Do you think you'd have healthy relationships with them?

Our heavenly Father wants a relationship with us that is real and personal. He's a willing participant. How willing are we to make time for Him? How often do we call on God only when we're in trouble or feel we need something? Do we have a "don't call me, I'll call you" attitude? God doesn't push Himself on us. He has given us free will and lets us choose; however, if we're willing to make time for Him, He's always available.

So how do we make time for Him? Having a daily quiet time is a discipline. Just as we'd never dream of leaving the house without brushing our teeth, we shouldn't go a day without making time for God.

But what exactly is a daily quiet time? Simply put, a quiet time consists of moments you spend with God. This time would include praying, writing in a prayer journal, reading the Bible, and listening for the voice of God. Do not feel you must be ritualistic or formal. Just spend time with God as you would with a friend. Get to know Him and tell Him about yourself; don't only make requests.

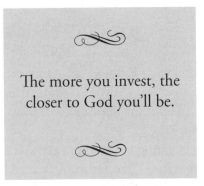

The more you invest, the closer to God you'll be.

I know some women who spend hours each day in quiet time with Jesus. Unlike me, they are not raising small children. You will find that your stage in life will impact how much time you're able to commit to your quiet time. Realize, though, that the more you invest, the closer to God you'll be. Ironically,

GREENSBORO AREA

DOROTHY NANCE STRAYER

GREENSBORO — Dorothy Nance Strayer, 89, passed away on November 28, 2010. Mrs. Strayer was a life long residence of Guilford County born to James Franklin and Lillie Mae Vaughan Nance. She worked as an Office Manager for Dental Practice.

The Graveside Memorial Service with be held on Saturday, December 4, at 11 a.m. at Guilford Memorial Park in Greensboro.

Mrs. Strayer was preceded in death by her parents; her husband, Rush Strayer; a sister, Helen Murray; and a brother James Nance.

Mrs. Strayer is survived by her daughter, Deborah Rush Strayer; three sisters, Millicent McCoy, Eloise Wood, and Louise Lowdermilk; and a brother Fred Nance.

There will be no visitation and memorials can be made to the American Heart Association, 202 Centreport Drive, Greensboro, 27409.

Lambeth-Troxler Funeral Service is assisting the family through this time of grieve. 6-1-11 #566

Online Condolences may be made to www.lambethtroxler-funeralhome.com. 50.00

ditorials, go to www.news-record.com

the time when I feel I need God the most is the time when I possibly have the least amount of free time. My quiet time must become a priority in order for it to happen.

As with anything new, it will take a while for your quiet time to work its way into your life as a habit. Start small so you can feel successful. If you're currently not doing anything on a daily basis, begin by committing just ten minutes a day to Bible reading and prayer. After you've mastered this, you can start increasing your time. Perhaps you can use those ten minutes for reading one chapter of Psalms (or another book of the Bible) and then spending the remaining time in prayer. If you're a little uncomfortable about praying, use a journal and write prayers to God as if you were writing Him a letter. Ask God to help you in your commitment and give you an increased desire to read His word and spend time with Him.

Work this ten-minute quiet time into your daily routine—just like brushing your teeth. To cement your new habit, try to participate in your quiet time at the same time each day. Lots of people feel it's great to have a quiet time in the morning because it helps start the day by focusing on the Lord. For you, though, it may not be realistic or practical to set aside time first thing in the morning. The important thing is that you find a time and a place that works for you. One word of caution: you may not want to plan your quiet time as the last thing you do in the day. Reclining in bed reading your Bible is a sure prescription for sleep. If your only available time is at night, sit in a place where you won't fall asleep or be distracted. God deserves our best, not our leftovers.

Other ideas for opportunities for quiet times include your lunch hour or a break at work. If you commute to work using public transportation, you could use that time to read your Bible or listen to Christian CDs. (Public libraries often have a copy of the Bible on audiocassettes or CDs.)

A final word about establishing a quiet time is to consider setting up accountability measures. Make a note on your calendar each month to evaluate how you're doing with your quiet time. That way, months don't pass you by if you get off track. Also, consider finding an accountability partner. This person might check in with you daily or weekly to see how well you're sticking to your commitment. Be creative and do what it takes. It will be well worth your effort.

God Says:

- "For where your treasure is, there your heart will be also. . . . No one can serve two masters. Either he will hate the one and love the other, or he will be devoted to the one and despise the other. You cannot serve both God and Money" (Matt. 6:21, 24).
- "Can a mother forget the baby at her breast and have no compassion on the child she has borne? Though she may forget, I will not forget you! See, I have engraved you on the palms of my hands" (Isa. 49:15–16).
- "Now if we are children, then we are heirs—heirs of God and co-heirs with Christ, if indeed we share in his sufferings in order that we may also share in his glory" (Rom. 8:17).
- "Jesus replied, 'If anyone loves me, he will obey my teaching. My Father will love him, and we will come to him and make our home with him'" (John 14:23).
- "As the Father has loved me, so have I loved you. Now remain in my love. If you obey my commands, you will remain in my love, just as I have obeyed my Father's commands and remain in his love. I have told you this so that my joy may be in you and that your joy may be complete" (John 15:9–11).

- "Greater love has no one than this, that he lay down his life for his friends. You are my friends if you do what I command. I no longer call you servants, because a servant does not know his master's business. Instead, I have called you friends, for everything that I learned from my Father I have made known to you. You did not choose me, but I chose you and appointed you to go and bear fruit—fruit that will last. Then the Father will give you whatever you ask in my name" (John 15:13–16).
- "I will walk among you and be your God, and you will be my people" (Lev. 26:12).
- "Truly our fellowship is with the Father and with His Son Jesus Christ" (1 John 1:3 KJ21).
- "Those who obey his commands live in him, and he in them. And this is how we know that he lives in us: We know it by the Spirit he gave us" (1 John 3:24).
- "Remain in me, and I will remain in you. No branch can bear fruit by itself; it must remain in the vine. Neither can you bear fruit unless you remain in me" (John 15:4).
- "Here I am! I stand at the door and knock. If anyone hears my voice and opens the door, I will come in and eat with him, and he with me" (Rev. 3:20).

Your Chance to Dance:

- Make a daily date with God. Find a quiet place where you can be alone. Take your Bible and a journal or notepad for writing what God reveals to you.
- The next time you're about to call a friend for advice, stop and take five minutes to pray and seek God's guidance first.
- Find an accountability partner—someone who's willing to check with you daily to see if you've had your quiet time with the Lord.

- Plan a day or weekend retreat. Spend time with Him like you would a good friend.
- Pray that God will help you find a godly mentor to encourage you in your journey with Him.

Chapter Six

GOD IS ENOUGH

*W*hen *I heard the words, "Your baby has a fatal chromo-*
somal defect and will most likely die before birth," I was
speechless—shocked almost to numbness. I struggled to process the
words. How could this be? I've had two healthy babies already.
This wasn't supposed to happen. This only happens to other people.
Reality set in and I think I cried for two solid days. The dreary
March weather, rainy and cold, fit my mood. I'd been hit with the
worst news of my life. How would I survive?

When faced with painful circumstances we respond in
many ways. We may withdraw and slip into denial. We may
try to find answers to how we arrived at this point. We may
try to place blame or alleviate pain. Ultimately though, we
have to deal with the issue at hand and somehow we begin
to cope.

Whether it's a shocking event that takes time to digest or a
slow downward spiral, it's easy to become discouraged when
we face hardships. Our emotional pain may be so consuming
that it spills over into the physical. We may feel alone in our
circumstances—like no one understands. If we've experienced
a loss, such as the death of a loved one, or the loss of health, a

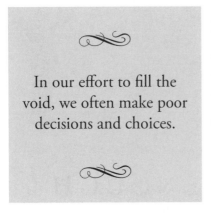

> In our effort to fill the void, we often make poor decisions and choices.

job, or a spouse via divorce, we may have an intense need to fill the void that's left. Beware. In our effort to fill the void, we often make poor decisions and choices. We engage in another relationship, find comfort in unhealthy behaviors such as overeating or drinking alcohol, or engage in some other compulsive behavior such as gambling or shopping. Nothing can fill the emptiness or loss except Jesus.

God's Comfort

"Be still, and know that I am God" (Ps. 46:10). I feel a sense of awe whenever I read this verse. He is *God*—mighty, powerful, loving, and in charge of all the heavens and the earth. What a comfort to be reminded that God is in total control. He is bigger than any problem I have and can save me from anything. Anything! God's Word is filled with promises of comfort for us in times of trouble; however, we often forget to turn there to search for the help we need. We pray, we talk to our friends, we read spiritually based books, but we forget to read the Bible. The Bible is God's Word and it's His primary way of speaking to us, so if we're in need of hearing from God and feeling His comfort, it's the best place to start. Second Corinthians 1:3 says He is "the Father of compassion and the God of all comfort."

God's comfort became an immediate need, once again, nine months after we lost Ashlynn. Mother's Day was coming and for the entire previous month, I had bizarre dreams and very restless nights. During the day I was preoccupied and unsettled. After much wrestling and soul searching, I concluded that all of my unrest was being caused by my anxiety over a fifteen-minute event that would soon be occurring in church.

Every year on Mother's Day our church holds a baby dedication ceremony. If Ashlynn were alive, we would have been participating in the celebration. A million thoughts and questions ran through my mind. *What dress would we have picked for her? Would she have cooperated during the service or would we be passing her back and forth trying to keep her quiet? Would she have been content pulling on my necklace or the button on my blouse? Would she have been trying to play with the pink carnation we'd be holding?*

I'll never know the answers to those questions. All I know is that I was in agony because we'd be missing out on that special day with our daughter. Even though I made sense of my feelings, I was still very frustrated. If I could pinpoint my issue, why couldn't I overcome it? Even more frustrating was the fact that the very thing I was upset about wasn't even relevant. The whole point of a baby dedication for Ashlynn had already been accomplished in her life. She was in heaven with Jesus for eternity! As a Christian parent, that's my ultimate goal for my children, and for Ashlynn, that had been achieved.

So then why was I still agonizing about this fifteen-minute ceremony? I tried getting the church to help me in my grief. I put unrealistic expectations on my husband, wanting him to fix my pain. Nothing worked. Even if the others had been willing to help me, they would have only provided Band-Aids®. Ultimately, I needed to dig deep to the core issue and release it to God.

That release to God finally happened. I went for a walk one day and began wrestling with my thoughts as I exercised. I began to pray about my struggle with the upcoming baby dedication ceremony. As I finally poured out my heart to Him and said, "I can't do this," He responded. Tears ran down my face as I sensed God gently reminding me that He could handle my pain even if I couldn't. I had to turn it over to Him—only He could heal my broken heart. I finally admitted defeat, and what a relief it was! I didn't have to carry the weight around anymore and I didn't have to be followed by the dark cloud that had been hovering. A friend wrote these words to me after I shared my struggles with her about the baby dedication:

> Though I can't possibly relate in full to what you will be feeling, once I got home, I, too, felt sad imagining how I would feel in your place. It struck me that God will be even more in touch with how you are feeling, since He now holds your sweet Ashlynn in His arms and knows her unconditional love, perfect in every way. He has baptized her in His arms. I got to thinking about what a holy time it will be for you, in that God will be attending *you and your daughter* at the same time. I'm getting a picture, and I'm sure He is giving you a uniquely special picture in your mind to treasure until you meet her again.

When I originally read my friend's note, I remember thinking, *I sure hope I get a special picture, but I'm not there yet.* Now as I reflect on it again, it is indeed a treasure that God is the connection between Ashlynn and me. She will always be a part of my life. Although we live in different realms, God is a constant for both of us and we will always share that. He is always present and loves us both. There is great comfort in knowing that.

Your pain may be related to something else—a broken friendship, loneliness, an unhappy marriage, struggles with your children, financial problems, or chronic pain. God's promises and comfort hold true for you, too. Jeremiah cries out, "Ah, Sovereign Lord, you have made the heavens and the earth by your great power and outstretched arm. Nothing is too hard for you" (Jer. 32:17). Think about it. The same God who created this universe and everything in it also created you and me. He simply spoke things into being. He made the sun stop for a day for Joshua. He parted the Red Sea. Don't you think He can mend our hurts and hold our hand as He guides us through our struggles? He's just waiting for us to ask. Think of Him like a loving father who is just waiting for you to climb into His arms for a hug.

I shared earlier about the woman hugging me as I cried out to God. As I opened myself up to Him, He met my needs. If you're willing to love Him and give yourself to Him, He will comfort you, too.

Another image that helps me understand the depth of God's love and His ability to comfort comes from Isaiah 40:11, "He tends his flock like a shepherd: He gathers the lambs in his arms and carries them close to his heart." Can you picture be-

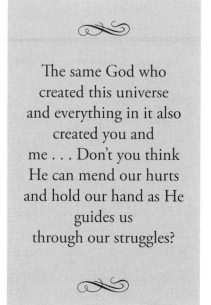

The same God who created this universe and everything in it also created you and me . . . Don't you think He can mend our hurts and hold our hand as He guides us through our struggles?

ing carried in His arms, close to His heart? He can comfort you no matter how great the hurt. The 23rd Psalm is probably one of the most popular passages in the Bible. Many churches teach it to their children through rote memorization. Even if you can recite it from memory, take a closer look at it below. Read each line deliberately and really digest its meaning.

> "The Lord is my shepherd, I shall not be in want.
> He makes me lie down in green pastures, he leads
> me beside quiet waters, he restores my soul. He
> guides me in paths of righteousness for his name's

sake. Even though I walk through the valley of the shadow of death, I will fear no evil, for you are with me; your rod and your staff, they comfort me. You prepare a table before me in the presence of my enemies. You anoint my head with oil; my cup overflows. Surely goodness and love will follow me all the days of my life, and I will dwell in the house of the LORD forever."

(Ps. 23:1–6)

This passage shows God's goodness and His love for us. He is our caregiver, providing for all our needs. He gives us rest and restores our souls. Take a moment and really imagine what is described in the first verse. Think of lush green grass, a quiet lake with perhaps a gentle breeze. Imagine the sounds: the gentle lapping of water, birds chirping, the soft whisper of the wind. Imagine the warm sun on your face, quiet and still. I can feel refreshed just by taking a quiet moment, closing my eyes, and imagining this scene. How beautiful and peaceful it is.

God promises comfort during times of trial. He promises safety from our enemies. He promises the gift of dwelling with Him forever in eternity. All these promises are for His followers. The closer we are to Him in communication and obedience, the greater level of comfort and peace we will find even in the midst of turmoil.

His Presence

A recurring theme throughout my grief has been my sense of being alone. I could be in a room filled with fifty people I knew and still feel alone. At times it was surreal, as if I was watching certain events from afar even though I knew I was actually in the middle of them. Whether it was real or not, I even felt that many of my friends had deserted me.

I wasn't able to adequately convey my needs, and most people aren't comfortable dealing with death. I would talk to other mothers who'd experienced the death of a child and discovered that their feelings and experiences were quite different from mine in many ways. Again, I felt alone. I was very reflective over the months and was trying to process my thoughts and emotions.

Over time, and after much prayer, I discovered that God wanted me to focus on Him. Had I not experienced the feeling of being alone, I likely wouldn't have turned to Him. I would have relied on friends and family. Instead, through Bible study and daily devotions I repeatedly read verses about seeking Him and relying on Him. My thoughts became saturated with scriptural truths. Perhaps He was trying to show me that He is always enough in every situation and nothing is too big for Him. All in all, He simply wanted my attention. He didn't want me leaning on my friends or family; He wanted me leaning on Him. He wanted to be the one to whom I'd pour out my heart. He wanted to be my everything. I began to learn from experience what I had always believed—that God is always present; however, I often didn't feel His love and compassion until I cried out to Him. Once I asked, He revealed Himself and made His presence known in very real ways. Unfortunately, I was a slow learner in this area and frequently reverted to old habits. I would go back to relying on others and would end up feeling alone again. Then I'd cry out, and again He'd make His presence known.

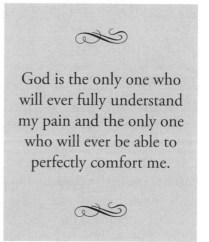

God is the only one who will ever fully understand my pain and the only one who will ever be able to perfectly comfort me.

God is the only one who will ever fully understand my pain and the only one who will ever be able to perfectly comfort me. That's not to say that He won't use people around me to accomplish it, but ultimately, it's His presence that satisfies. I believe that applies to any hardship.

Psalm 46:1 says, "God is our refuge and strength, an ever-present help in trouble." He is always there. He's never too busy. He's never looking the other way. He's never uninterested. He is always present. He tells us that He has engraved us on the palms of His hands (Isa. 49:16). Does it get any better than that?

God is always at work around us. He didn't speak our creation into being, set the world in motion, and then check out for a while. He knows every flower, every bird, every ocean, every grain of sand, and yes, every person. We were created in His image. He deliberately made us and He's always with us. As Christians, we're filled with the Holy Spirit—He is *in* us.

So if He's in us and around us, then why do we act and feel like He's not? This is the million dollar question. Perhaps we take our eyes off Him and become consumed with worldly things. Or maybe we step up and take charge instead of seeking God's best for us. There have certainly been times that I've struggled to sense God's presence. I know that He's there, but at times it doesn't feel like it. I can look at nature around me and know that He created it, or I can see how He orchestrated certain events or situations to work out in a way that benefits His family of believers, but even though I see it, at times I just don't feel it.

In recent years, I've heard two different descriptions of God that have helped me explain His presence to my children. These descriptions have also helped me to grasp the concept myself. The first example is the wind. We can't see the wind. We can't catch it, bottle it, contain it, or control it; however, we know it's real. The wind can be calm, gentle, and refreshing, or it can be quite powerful. Even if the air is still and we don't feel the wind, no one can argue that it doesn't exist.

The other example compares God to airwaves. Think about radio. Radio waves are always being transmitted even when our radio is turned off. We have to be tuned in to a specific channel to receive the signal and receive any kind of intelligible sound. Likewise, God is always here; however, sometimes we're tuned into a different station and we miss the blessing of His presence.

Are you experiencing the richness of His presence or are you tuned to another station? My experience has been that when we're hurting, we either draw nearer to God or push Him away. We may not intentionally push Him away, but we do it in subtle ways. We consult our friends for guidance, instead of the Bible. We want those close to us to help us feel better instead of praying for God to reveal Himself and rescue us. We become consumed with worry and anxiety. We

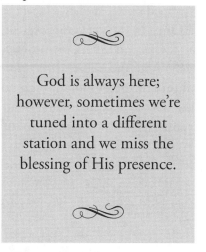

God is always here; however, sometimes we're tuned into a different station and we miss the blessing of His presence.

may be angry with God, even screaming at Him or refusing to acknowledge Him. Whatever the case, if we're not tuned in to Him, we miss the opportunity to experience the best He has for us.

His Strength

As I got closer to my due date, the anticipation grew. With each doctor's visit, I'd wonder what the ultrasound would reveal. Each time had been encouraging and Ashlynn was thriving. Although she was small, she was growing at a steady rate. Then came the dreaded day. Her condition was starting to deteriorate and the doctor felt it was time to induce labor. To say I was petrified would be an understatement. I didn't want to be induced. I wanted her to arrive in God's timing because that would remove any decision-making on my part.

I vividly remember that afternoon. As I left the doctor's office, I was certainly a driving hazard, as I could barely see through the stream of tears. I was desperate. I had to get to the nearest McDonald's® for some comfort food. (This is our little secret. You see, I'm a dietitian by trade and if word gets out, I could be stripped of my credentials and have my registration revoked.)

Once in the drive-through lane, I composed myself enough so the person taking my order could understand that I needed a Big Mac and a Diet Coke®. I'd been living a deprived life as a dutiful pregnant mother—no caffeine or artificial sweeteners as the doctors had instructed—but this crisis had pushed me beyond my limits. I couldn't go into the restaurant to eat because everyone would see me crying, so I sat in the parking lot and stuffed my face with my fat-laden, sauce-dripping sandwich.

Right there in the car I literally cried out to God and told Him that He'd chosen the wrong person to which to give this trial.

> If God decides not to deliver us from whatever ails us, He'll give us the strength to get through it.

I reminded Him of all my weaknesses and suggested that He take a good look at me. Clearly I was a mess! What could He possibly be thinking?

In all His grace and goodness, He replied directly to me from His word, "Fear not, for I am with you; be not dismayed, for I am your God. I will strengthen you, yes, I will help you, I will uphold you with My righteous right hand" (Isa. 41:10 NKJV). He assured me of His strength. Although it was clear that I couldn't face this hardship on my own, He reminded me that I can do anything through Christ who strengthens me (Phil. 4:13).

If God decides not to deliver us from whatever ails us, He'll give us the strength to get through it. Again, the key is tapping into His source of power and strength.

I was recently reminded of a great visual in Habakkuk 3:19, "The Sovereign LORD is my strength; he makes my feet like the feet of a deer, he enables me to go on the heights." That verse had never had great meaning for me until I recalled an incident involving a deer that happened a few years earlier.

The area surrounding my neighborhood includes both open fields and woods. As I was driving down the main road one morning, I saw a deer running through the field toward the road. At first I didn't give it much thought, but he didn't seem to be slowing down and was running directly toward the road. I could tell that the deer was either going to collide with my car or with the car in front of me. I held my breath and braced for the collision. I was astonished at what happened next. Without ever breaking stride, the deer leapt over the car and disappeared through the trees on the other side of the road.

Perhaps it's a well-known fact that deer can jump like that, but I must have been taking a nap that day in school. Or perhaps the actual sight of it just made a great impact. Either way, after witnessing that deer's leap, the verse in Habakkuk now has much greater meaning to me. I want to be an overcomer like that deer. If he can leap over a car that's traveling fifty miles per hour, then I want to have feet like his.

What are you struggling to overcome? Are you struggling as a single mother? Are you battling feelings of dissatisfaction with life? Are you trying to overcome an addiction? Ask God to be your strength and give you feet like a deer. He'll take you to new heights.

Hope

Somehow I came to have hope that Ashlynn would be born alive; however, I wasn't sure how much time I'd have with her. I was scheduled to be induced at 7:00 on a Friday morning. I don't recall my exact feelings that morning, but I'm sure I experienced a combination of excitement and fear similar to my previous birthing experiences. Only this time, there was the added dimension of caution because of Ashlynn's condition.

I had made arrangements with Jessica, a local photographer who volunteered for a national organization called Now I Lay Me Down to Sleep, to be there as soon as Ashlynn arrived. I figured I had everything set, but more unknowns than I had ever expected popped up that day.

During the early stages of labor, a steady stream of guests came and went through my room. At one point, I had to threaten to have the nurses remove my mom and mother-in-law because they were having a bit too much fun watching my labor pains on the computer monitor beside my bed. I had not had any pain medications, so I was very aware of my contractions regardless of what they saw on the monitor. Things had been moving slowly, so when they saw a large spike on the graph on the computer screen, they began to cheer. Picture the two of them looking at the computer beside me, jumping up and down as I writhed in pain. Had there been something available to throw at them, I would have.

Suddenly, things took a turn for the worse. The nurse and doctor came rushing in. "It's time to get her out. We're prepping you for a C-section." At this, I fell apart. I desperately wanted to avoid a C-section. Worse yet, I knew this meant Ashlynn was not doing well. As the doctors called for the anesthesiologist, they sent me to the restroom one last time. I was sobbing and trembling with fear. *What if she's doesn't make it? The moment is here. Will I survive?* I could barely see through the tears when I happened to look up at the wall beside me. There was a rather large medallion hanging on the wall with the word "HOPE" etched in its center. It was as if God was trying to shake me out of my fear-stricken state and say, "Focus on Me."

Amazingly, I was able to calm down. Still facing the unknown, I composed myself and headed back into the room. Within minutes I'd know if my daughter would enter this world dead or alive. God truly was my only hope and I was hanging on for dear life.

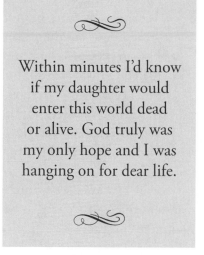

Within minutes I'd know if my daughter would enter this world dead or alive. God truly was my only hope and I was hanging on for dear life.

Although my hope in that situation was that God would do what I wanted Him to, there's actually a much greater hope that we're called to in the Bible. God wants us to push past placing our hope only on things that are temporal. Ultimately, our hope should rest in things eternal—hope in what He wants for us, not necessarily what we think we want at the time.

Romans 15:13 reminds us that He is the God of hope and that we'll be filled with joy and peace as we trust in Him. Knowing this, I pondered Isaiah 49:23, "Those who hope in me will not be disappointed," and I struggled to comprehend what God had in store for me. I had to believe that even though His plan was for me to be separated from Ashlynn, He had something better in store. Perhaps I won't find out what that is until I'm in heaven, but I'll never be disappointed as I place my hope in God, because He's given me eternal life and an inheritance to look forward to.

In Lamentations 3:21–26, we're given a great example of how to find hope in the midst of affliction:

> Yet this I call to mind
> and therefore I have hope:
> Because of the LORD's great love we are not consumed,
> for his compassions never fail.
> They are new every morning;
> great is your faithfulness.
> I say to myself, "The LORD is my portion;
> therefore I will wait for him."
> The LORD is good to those whose hope is in him,
> to the one who seeks him;
> It is good to wait quietly
> for the salvation of the LORD.

Trust in His love, seek Him and wait for Him. He always comes through. "Be joyful in hope, patient in affliction, faithful in prayer" (Rom. 12:12).

His Provisions

The Bible gives us glimpses of how God provides for His people. For example, in the Old Testament, He provided manna for the Israelites during their journey to the Promised Land and food for Elijah during famine and drought. In the New Testament, Jesus miraculously fed thousands of people on several occasions, and He provided wine at a wedding feast.

God still provides for His people today. Whether it is for physical needs or emotional ones, God provides. There are three things to remember about His provisions: first, He sometimes asks for our participation; second, He often provides differently than we expect; and third, He sometimes provides just enough, instead of excess. Let's look at examples of each of these.

God used Peter's participation in Acts 12 when Peter was miraculously released from prison. An angel appeared, woke Peter, and then his chains fell off. The angel instructed him, "Put on your clothes and sandals. . . . Wrap your cloak around you and follow me" (v. 8). Peter passed the guards, and the iron gate opened by itself.

You see, Peter had a role in the escape. He had to recognize God's angel, trust the instructions, and make the choice to follow. You might think that it was a "no brainer"—what other options did he have? Still, Peter's participation to fully bring about God's provision was an act of faith. He would have surely been put to death if he'd been caught trying to escape.

God was capable of taking care of the entire act without Peter's participation. God could have simply zapped Peter out of the jail and plopped him down in the midst of the room where the believers were praying for him. Why did Peter need to participate?

God provides us with opportunities to build our faith. The only way God can help us eliminate fear is to allow us to exercise faith. Just as Peter had to get dressed (i.e., prepare himself) and follow God's guidance, we are often called to participate in God's leading. Are you ready and willing? If so, you may find that God readily provides.

God's provision doesn't always come as we expect.

Secondly, God's provision doesn't always come as we expect. He often provides differently than we anticipate. As the Savior of the world, Jesus is the perfect example of this point.

The people of that time were expecting a warrior king to save them, not a humble, gentle man who arrived as a lowly baby. Because of God's unexpected provision, many people rejected

Jesus during His ministry. In Acts 2 we learn that it wasn't until after His death that thousands of people came to accept Christ as the Messiah.

I'm reminded of times I thought God wasn't answering my prayers when in reality He was and I just didn't recognize it at the time. You often hear people say that something was a blessing in disguise. I think there's truth in that statement. In the midst of trials or difficult situations, it's sometimes hard to see that God knows better than we do. We may not understand at the moment why something is happening. It's not until later that we realize God was working things out in His way and His timing.

Finally, we see that God's provision is always enough. In Exodus 16, God sent manna to feed the Israelites. They were instructed to gather only as much as they needed. They were given specific instructions not to try to save any of the manna because God had plans to provide for their needs each day. Those who disobeyed found that the manna they saved was filled with maggots and foul odors.

Instead of giving us excess, God sometimes provides "just enough" to meet our needs. In today's culture of wealth and overabundance, our nature seems to be to store up for whatever we may need in the future; however, this reveals an attitude of self-reliance rather than one of dependence upon God. God assures us that we're more valuable than flowers, trees, and sparrows, and since He provides for them, we can be sure that He'll certainly provide for us. Are we willing to trust Him?

His Lifeline

During my pregnancy, as I went to each subsequent doctor's visit, Ashlynn was continuing to grow and survive against the odds. Although we could see on ultrasound that she didn't have the necessary chambers of her heart and she had deformities of her hands and feet, I was oblivious to it day to day. I knew those issues existed, but I felt the kicks, pushes, and turns of my sweet baby girl. People in the world around me saw a pregnant woman and had no idea of my baby's health issues.

As my delivery date approached, it occurred to me that second to God, I was Ashlynn's lifeline. I was providing her nutrients and all necessary life-sustaining elements. She was growing and thriving inside me. She was active and seemed to have her own personality. Even though she was sick, she was the most feisty of any of my children while in utero. She kicked and moved with the greatest force and was always active and uncooperative when the technicians did the ultrasounds. She would roll and turn while they patiently tried to get the views they needed. She was definitely alive. I would talk to her throughout the day and gently rub or pat my belly when she was active.

Likewise, God was sustaining me. I'm not sure what I would have done without the presence and strength of God. I'm certain that would have been a very bad place in which to be. I have never felt closer to God than during my pregnancy with Ashlynn, and I can't explain the peace that He gave me.

I loved Ashlynn with all my heart, but the day would come when she'd be separated from me and because of her condition would no longer be able to survive apart from me. I have found that my relationship with God is very similar. He is my lifeline. Without Him, I am incomplete. Jesus tells us, "Remain in me, and I will remain in you. No branch can bear fruit by itself; it must remain in the vine. Neither can you bear fruit unless you remain in me. I am the vine; you are the branches. If a man remains in me and I in him, he will bear much fruit; apart from me you can do nothing" (John 15:4–5).

Without my lifeline, my life is meaningless. Prior to now, much of my life was about acquiring "stuff." I wouldn't say that I worshipped money or material things; however, they were prioritized higher than they should have been. I now have a very different perspective of life—one that others often don't understand. I think and feel differently. I have different priorities. I have more thoughts of eternity and my role in God's kingdom while I'm here on earth. I recognize that apart from Him, my life is meaningless.

> We can find true fulfillment and experience God's best for us only when we're closely linked to the source of life.

Where are you in your journey in this life? Are you connected to God's lifeline or are you drifting through life wondering about your purpose and meaning? We can find true fulfillment and experience God's best for us only when we're closely linked to the source of life. As we allow Him to work in our lives, show us His perspective, and follow His leading, we'll experience a peace beyond all understanding.

His Grace

The Merriam-Webster® online dictionary defines grace as "unmerited divine assistance given humans for their regeneration or sanctification" and "a virtue coming from God."[1] Notice that grace is unmerited. I've often heard it described as getting something wonderful that you didn't earn or deserve. Yet God gives us divine assistance for the purpose of sanctification, i.e. making us holy or setting us apart.

Although biblical scholars disagree on the exact nature of the thorn in Paul's side, we know that Paul asked God repeatedly to remove it. God chose not to, and instead told Paul that His grace was sufficient for Paul (2 Cor. 12:7–10). This makes me think of the old adage, "If God brings you to it, He'll bring you through it." We may not like the situations God allows in our lives, but He assures us that He can help us endure or overcome them.

I've had many struggles as I've dealt with Ashlynn's death; however, God has always been there to help me each step of the way. There are some things I may never resolve, but I have to trust that God's grace is sufficient for me. Even now, I dread it and continue to struggle

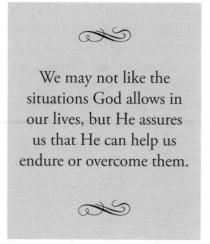

We may not like the situations God allows in our lives, but He assures us that He can help us endure or overcome them.

whenever someone asks me the question, "How many children do you have?" If I don't include Ashlynn in the count, I feel like I'm dishonoring her or somehow trying to pretend she didn't exist. If I do include her, the person inevitably asks about the ages of my kids and I feel I have to give an explanation. Then there's an awkward moment or silence for which I feel responsible. I don't want people to feel sorry for me, and sometimes I just don't feel like sharing. I also don't want to be defined as the poor woman whose baby died. Yes, Ashlynn died and it was a defining experience. I was thrust into a "club" of which I didn't want to be a member. To confound the issues of this internal conflict, I know that my children are watching and listening to what I say. Do they understand why sometimes I tell people about Ashlynn and sometimes I don't? My oldest daughter has corrected me before when I was talking to the cashier at the grocery store. She clearly wanted me to tell about Ashlynn.

Recently, someone asked me how many children I had and I responded that I had two children. (This was after Ashlynn's death, but prior to my pregnancy with my son.) Not knowing my whole story, she went on to jokingly say that I'm smart not to have three children like her because it's a lot of work. I wanted to scream. I wasn't angry with her. She didn't know my situation, but her comment evoked a great deal of emotion in me. I refrained from saying anything because I didn't want to make her feel bad. The other woman standing with us knew my circumstances and turned away when the comment was made. I think she sensed how difficult it was for me to hear and she was uncomfortable.

Some people think there's a clear and simple answer to my dilemma, but I've yet to resolve it. Maybe over time, situations like these will become less frequent and evoke less emotion; however, I'm sure there will be times that catch me by surprise and dig deep into the soul. At such times, I'll need to remember God's source of strength, comfort, love, and grace.

Have you been inducted to a club to which you didn't want to belong? Perhaps it was the cancer club, or the divorced club, or the widow's club. Will you trust God to be enough for you? I challenge you to turn your eyes toward Him and let Him be your heart's true desire. He can fill every void in your heart if you let Him.

God Says:

- "Have I not commanded you? Be strong and courageous. Do not be terrified; do not be discouraged, for the LORD your God will be with you wherever you go" (Josh. 1:9).
- "'For I know the plans I have for you,' declares the LORD, 'plans to prosper you and not to harm you, plans to give you hope and a future'" (Jer. 29:11).
- "Never will I leave you; never will I forsake you" (Heb. 13:5).
- "The LORD is near to all who call on him, to all who call on him in truth" (Ps. 145:18).

- "My comfort in my suffering is this: Your promise preserves my life" (Ps. 119:50).
- "As a mother comforts her child, so will I comfort you" (Isa. 66:13).
- "Do not let your hearts be troubled. Trust in God; trust also in me" (John 14:1).
- "Praise be to the God and Father of our Lord Jesus Christ, the Father of compassion and the God of all comfort" (2 Cor. 1:3).
- "Cast all your anxiety on him because he cares for you" (1 Pet. 5:7).
- "For who is God besides the LORD? And who is the Rock except our God? It is God who arms me with strength and makes my way perfect. He makes my feet like the feet of a deer; he enables me to stand on the heights" (Ps. 18:31–33).
- "The LORD gives strength to his people; the LORD blesses his people with peace" (Ps. 29:11).
- "Look to the LORD and his strength; seek his face always" (Ps. 105:4).
- "The LORD is my strength and my song; he has become my salvation" (Ps. 118:14).
- "My soul is weary with sorrow; strengthen me according to your word" (Ps. 119:28).
- "He gives strength to the weary and increases the power of the weak" (Isa. 40:29).
- "But those who hope in the LORD will renew their strength. They will soar on wings like eagles; they will run and not grow weary, they will walk and not be faint" (Isa. 40:31).
- "From the fullness of his grace we have all received one blessing after another" (John 1:16).
- "And God is able to make all grace abound to you, so that in all things at all times, having all that you need, you will abound in every good work" (2 Cor. 9:8).

Your Chance to Dance:

- Read the book of Job in the Bible. Make a list of all the things he endured while remaining faithful to God.
- Think about your current level of satisfaction with your life. Is God your focus or are you seeking other things? List ways you could redirect your path back to God.
- What is your greatest emotional need right now (examples: acceptance, love, security, encouragement)? List ways God could meet these needs. Are you willing to allow Him to fill the void in your life instead of seeking others?
- Memorize scriptures that demonstrate God's ability to meet your physical, spiritual, and emotional needs. (Search scriptures by keywords using an online Bible site such as www.biblegateway.com.)
- Make a set of note cards with the verses of God's promises for comfort, presence, strength, hope, and provision. Keep the set of cards with you in your purse, car, desk drawer, or night stand, and read them daily (more than once a day if necessary). You will soon commit these verses to memory and you'll be quick to bring them to mind in times of need.

Chapter Seven

ASK WHAT, NOT WHY

*W*hen I learned that our baby had trisomy 18—a death sentence—I had choices to make regarding my attitude. I could be miserable and angry throughout the rest of my pregnancy or I could enjoy the time I had with my child and thank God for her life. Ultimately, I wanted to bring honor and glory to Him. By choosing the latter, I ended up having the most amazing opportunity to know and love sweet Ashlynn and to grow closer to God than ever before in my life. I celebrated Ashlynn's life, and although saying goodbye to her was the hardest thing I've ever had to do, her life had such a profound impact on me that I'm forever changed. I saw the face of God through her. I saw His love, His hope, His faithfulness. I saw that as much as I loved her—imperfections and all—God also loves me—imperfections and all.

One of our natural responses to pain and suffering is to question why. Why is this happening to me? Why can't my life be different? Why does Nancy Neighbor always have good things happen while I struggle?

It's easy to get caught in the trap of asking why, but doing so leads to a downward spiral. We may never know why certain things happen. They may happen as a consequence of a decision or action we've taken. Tough circumstances may be a result of God trying to get our attention. He may be drawing us closer to Him, or He may be preparing us for something ahead. The list of possibilities is endless. If we spend our entire lives trying to determine why things happen, we're likely to miss the bigger picture and perhaps the bigger blessing.

Instead of constantly asking why, try asking God, "What do you want me to do?" or, "What do you want me to learn from this?" Not only will asking these questions make enduring the difficult time easier, but your new attitude will also set the atmosphere for a healthy perspective that invites growth and moving forward instead of getting stuck in the midst of the circumstances. As you seek God, you will find Him. He will reveal what He wants you to learn or do if you truly seek Him. This type of perspective benefits both you and God's kingdom. If we are consumed by our circumstances, we usually become ineffective for God. When we're so focused on ourselves and our challenges, we often aren't looking for ways to help others and aren't available for God's purposes. Yet, if we allow Him to work in us through difficult circumstances, the growth it produces can yield extraordinary fruit.

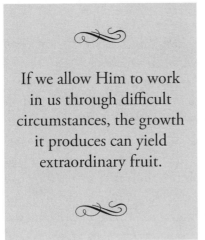

If we allow Him to work in us through difficult circumstances, the growth it produces can yield extraordinary fruit.

Have you ever known someone who questions everything? I once knew a woman who was apparently married to someone with such tendencies. She told me of a time when she ran out of her garage screaming, "Get the fire extinguisher!" Instead of immediately acting on her request, her husband responded, "Why?" Luckily, the fire was small and his delay didn't result in the destruction of the entire house, but it could have. Some things just shouldn't be questioned. Sometimes it is useful and appropriate to hesitate before you act, but lots of "whys" can be counterproductive if you don't use good judgment.

Like most us, I know people facing extremely difficult situations who are tempted to ask why. Consider the following situations:

- One dear family has a young child with a terminal illness. They watch as her health declines and as she struggles with her disabilities. They care for all her needs, never knowing when the end will come.
- There's the couple who desperately wants to have a child yet experiences repeated miscarriages instead.
- A young mom cares for her dying mother while trying to care for her young family. She knows her youngest child won't have memories of his grandparent.
- Then there's the family who's committed their lives to God, and instead of immediate blessing, their business fails and they lose their home.
- What about the young mother battling cancer who painfully watches her family wrestle with fear?

Do any of these situations sound like yours? There are lots of opportunities to ask God why. My heart breaks for each of these families, but I know there is hope.

All during my pregnancy, I continued to ask God to show me what He wanted, but after Ashlynn died, the inevitable occurred. As I went through the grieving process, I came to the point of being angry. Thankfully, the anger only lasted a short time, but during that time I began to ask God why. My other two kids were suffering from Ashlynn's death, and our family seemed a wreck. *What good could God possibly have had in mind? He must have made a mistake. Why did He make her this way? He could have healed her. That would have shown His power and glory! Why didn't he heal her? Why did He let her die?*

In the midst of my questioning and anger, God spoke to me from Isaiah 45:9–12:

> Woe to him who quarrels with his Maker, to him who is but a potsherd among the potsherds on the ground. Does the clay say to the potter, "What are you making?" Does your work say, "He has no hands"? Woe to him who says to his father, "What have you begotten?" or to his mother, "What have you brought to birth?" This is what the LORD says—the Holy One of Israel, and its Maker: Concerning things to come, do you question me about my children, or give me orders about the work of my hands? It is I who made the earth and created mankind upon it. My own hands stretched out the heavens; I marshaled their starry hosts.

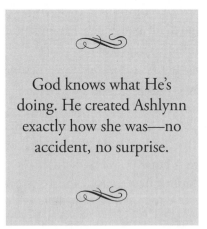

God knows what He's doing. He created Ashlynn exactly how she was—no accident, no surprise.

As I humbly stopped railing at God, I felt the need to change my words from "Why," to "Yes, sir." I got the point. God knows what He's doing. He created Ashlynn exactly how she was—no accident, no surprise. He had a plan for Ashlynn's life and she fulfilled her purpose here on this earth. I'm just glad that I was able to be a part of it.

The following story may be the only explanation we need when we're going through tough times:

> A women's Bible study group was studying the book of Malachi. They got to chapter 3, verse 3, which

says, "He will sit as a refiner and purifier of silver." This verse puzzled the women. They wondered what this statement meant about the character and nature of God. One of the women offered to find out about the process of refining silver and get back to the group at their next Bible study.

That week the woman called up a silversmith and made an appointment to watch him at work. She didn't mention anything about the reason for her interest in silver beyond her curiosity about the process of refining silver. As she watched, the silversmith held a piece of silver over the fire and let it heat up. He explained that in refining silver, one needed to hold the silver in the middle of the fire where the flames were hottest so as to burn away all the impurities.

The woman thought about God holding us in such a hot spot, then she thought again about the verse, "He will sit as a refiner and purifier of silver." She asked the silversmith, "Do you have to sit in front of the fire the whole time the silver is being refined?"

The man answered, "Yes, I not only have to sit here holding the silver, but I have to keep my eyes on the silver the entire time it is in the fire. If the silver is left even a moment too long in the flames, it will be destroyed."

The woman was silent for a moment. Then she asked the silversmith, "How do you know when the silver is fully refined?"

He smiled at her and answered, "Oh, that's easy. The silver is fully refined when I see my image in it."[1]

What a great picture of our heavenly Father refining us. He is always present, keeping His eye on us whatever we are going through. Although the process may be uncomfortable, the result is that we will come out bearing a greater reflection of His character. This should be our ultimate desire. We are created in God's image and should therefore desire to mirror His character. Since we're imperfect sinners, we often need to go through the refining process to remove impurities from our lives. He'll quite possibly take us to a deeper level in our relationship with Him through such refining.

Catalyst for Spiritual Growth

As I've changed my question from "Why, Lord?" to "What, Lord?" I've learned a lot about myself and my life. Change is slow, but I'm taking steps to do things differently in order to become the person I believe God wants me to be. Trusting God has been a big focus, as well as continuing to spend time in His Word and seek His direction for my life. I've also been compelled to try new things and look for opportunities to have fun and laugh, especially with my children. The saying "life is short" has a whole new meaning to me now and I want to make the most of each day by honoring God and enjoying life.

God sometimes uses hardships in our life to bring us back to Him.

Working through fear and not letting it control me or my decisions has also been an area of focus. In general, I now view things in the context of eternal rather than temporal importance. I'm thankful for the great revelation and new perspective, but I do have to work at not resorting to old thought patterns and habits.

God sometimes uses hardships in our life to bring us back to Him. We're told that all things work "for the good of those who love Him" (Rom. 8:28). Although we may not be able to see the good in a circumstance when we're in the midst of it, with enough prayer and thoughtfulness, we can often find something good that resulted from that difficult time.

As much as I don't want it to be true, the reality is that I was closest to God when I was at my lowest point in life. I was in agony over my circumstances, and that drove me to my knees. I was completely dependent on God throughout my pregnancy; however, as time passed, I felt myself drifting from God. I was going through the motions in my relationship with God and I missed the closeness I had once felt. I'm certain that I was drifting because I'd become more comfortable in my circumstances and less dependent on Him. More often than not, I was back in the driver's seat. I desperately wanted the closeness I once felt, but I was secretly scared that something bad would happen to force me back to God. I've had to repeatedly remind myself that God did not give me a spirit of fear. As I've wrestled with fear and worry, I always come to the same conclusion: neither of them is productive in my relationship with God. Fear and worry won't change anything; they simply waste precious energy and strength.

Although I had started to mature spiritually before Ashlynn was a part of my life, my spiritual life changed dramatically for the good when I learned of our circumstances. I had two choices: endure it with my own strength, or hang on tight to the Almighty God who promised to support me with His strength. My fear and suffering drove me to the path of seeking God with intense desire, not with just a casual glance. I wanted and needed to know Him. I wanted and needed His strength and love. He became my focus. In doing so, I was able to put my pain and suffering into the proper context. That's not to say that I didn't experience extreme sorrow, but

I always knew there was hope and that He would pull me through.

Are you experiencing something that seems unbearable? Or do you simply seem to fight the same battles day after day, feeling defeated and depleted? Sometimes it's the small things that rob us of our joy. Maybe worry creeps into your thoughts on a regular basis. Or maybe, no matter how hard you try, you lose your patience with those around you. By going deeper in your relationship with God, you'll not only experience a greater measure of His love and compassion, but you'll likely find that you start experiencing victory in other areas of your life.

Purpose and Meaning

Not long ago, I was watching *The Sound of Music* with my daughter and a quote from Captain von Trapp grabbed my attention. He said, "Activity suggests a life filled with purpose."[2] This is a nice-sounding sentiment, but I disagree. Activity can simply mean movement, not necessarily purpose. Much of society operates like this. Our feeling of importance seems to be measured by our degree of busyness, yet nothing could be further from the truth. I have often found my life so filled with activity that I no longer knew my purpose. Our activity is not purposeful unless we are following God's plan.

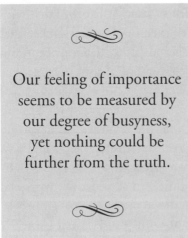

> Our feeling of importance seems to be measured by our degree of busyness, yet nothing could be further from the truth.

God has a plan for each of our lives, but it's up to us to decide if we're willing to seek His plan and submit to it. If we're so busy doing all the things *we* think are important, we'll likely miss God's real purpose for our lives and we won't live to our fullest potential. We'll also miss the real peace and contentment that comes from being in the will of God.

In addition to us each having a purpose in this life to expand God's kingdom, specific events and circumstances have purpose. Life is not a series of coincidences.

> If we're so busy doing all the things *we* think are important, we'll likely miss God's real purpose for our lives and we won't live to our fullest potential.

Every event, circumstance, and encounter happens for a reason. God can test us, as we learn in Isaiah. "See, I have refined you, though not as silver; I have tested you in the furnace of affliction" (Isa. 48:10). And sometimes things happen so God will be revealed and glorified. In the book of John, we're told the following story of a blind man. "As he went along, he saw a man blind from birth. His disciples asked him, 'Rabbi, who sinned, this man or his parents, that he was born blind?' 'Neither this man nor his parents sinned,' said Jesus, 'but this happened so that the work of God might be displayed in his life'" (John 9:1–3).

We are also instructed in James to "Consider it pure joy, my brothers, whenever you face trials of many kinds, because you know that the testing of your faith develops perseverance. Perseverance must finish its work so that you may be mature and complete, not lacking anything" (James 1:2–4).

What are you lacking that God is trying to grow and develop in you? What does He want you to learn from your current struggles? Are you willing to seek Him and learn from your trials? God assures us that "After you have suffered for a little while, the God of all grace, who called you to His eternal glory in Christ, will Himself perfect, confirm, strengthen and establish you" (1 Pet. 5:10 NASB).

Other times, God allows hardships so we'll be able to understand and help others. In 2 Corinthians 1:4 we are told that God "comforts us in all our troubles, so that we can comfort those in any trouble with the comfort we ourselves have received from God." I can completely relate, because now I can offer a different level of comfort and understanding to those suffering the loss of a loved one, especially the loss of a child. I can listen and speak from experience, not just make my best attempt to sympathize.

If we remember to give God the glory and use our hardships to share Jesus with others, we'll be richly blessed. "Restore our fortunes, O LORD, like streams in the Negev. Those who sow in tears will reap with songs of joy. He who goes out weeping, carrying seed to sow, will return with songs of joy, carrying sheaves with him" (Ps. 126:4–6). It's not easy to remain positive and praise God in the midst of painful circumstances, but He will reward you. Others will

It's not easy to remain positive and praise God in the midst of painful circumstances, but He will reward you.

take note of your attitude. Look for the opportunity to sow seeds for God's kingdom and you'll add meaning and purpose to your struggles. And when you find meaning and purpose, it's easier to endure pain and loss. Although it doesn't always seem possible, seek God for His wisdom and discernment.

ASK WHAT, NOT WHY

You may recall the story of Todd Beamer, known for heroic actions aboard United Airlines flight 93 on September 11, 2001. His wife Lisa suffered a great loss when his life tragically ended. She had two young sons at home and was pregnant with their daughter. Her family will never be the same. She immediately and unexpectedly became a single mother. Their daughter will never know her father and their youngest son may never remember him. I can only imagine her pain; however, she shares in her book *Let's Roll!* that the pain is more bearable knowing that her husband's life served a purpose and that his heroic actions saved the lives of others.

Otto Frank also comes to mind. Although he survived the horrors of the Holocaust, his wife, daughter, and other family members did not. He decided to publish his daughter's writings. *The Diary of Anne Frank* is a classic piece of literature that not only shares a piece of history, but gives meaning to his daughter's short life and suffering.

Seeking meaning and purpose can help us get through certain situations, but sometimes we just feel overwhelmed in the midst of it. Have you ever faced a daunting task that you knew was essentially impossible to accomplish? As the "room mom" for my daughter's dance class, I was given the task of dressing, organizing, and keeping fourteen six-year-old girls quiet while waiting for our turn during the dress rehearsal for the recital. And did I mention that they were all wearing tap shoes? At one point, I leaned close to one particularly active girl and pleaded for her to please stand still and lower her voice. She immediately started jumping up and down and yelled, "I'm too excited to be still!" I knew I was doomed because at least ten of the other girls shared her sentiment. There were two of us unsuspecting room moms . . . and fourteen of *them*. We were far outnumbered and clearly ill-equipped for the task at hand. Our only hope would be prayer.

Somehow we made it through the two-and-a-half-hour rehearsal and I was relieved of my duties until the next day at the recital. I was sweating, hungry, cross-eyed, and exhausted. I had been zapped of every ounce of energy, but I had survived.

Although this may be a humorous and insignificant example, it's not unlike many of life's challenges. The point was that I felt totally inadequate. I was fearful of failing my assigned task. I was overwhelmed as I realized the odds were not in my favor, yet I couldn't run and hide. I was committed. Ready or not, I had to do the best I could.

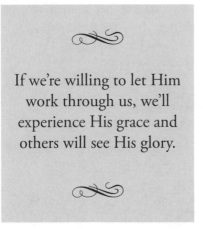

If we're willing to let Him work through us, we'll experience His grace and others will see His glory.

God will often ask us to do God-sized tasks. If we're willing to let Him work through us, we'll experience His grace and others will see His glory. Other times, He doesn't ask. We're just tossed into the situation. The way we choose to respond will determine the degree of peace we'll experience and blessings we'll receive. I'm not sure about you, but I'd rather look to see how God is going to use my hurts and challenges for something good than to waste precious energy repeatedly asking why. As I wait with anticipation and expectation, it's always a thrill to see God work His wonders.

God Says:

- "'For my thoughts are not your thoughts, neither are your ways my ways,' declares the LORD" (Isa. 55:8).
- "Look to the LORD and his strength; seek his face always" (Ps. 105:4).

- "'For I know the plans I have for you,' declares the LORD, 'plans to prosper you and not to harm you, plans to give you hope and a future'" (Jer. 29:11).
- "If any of you lacks wisdom, he should ask God, who gives generously to all without finding fault, and it will be given to him" (James 1:5).
- "For you, O God, tested us; you refined us like silver" (Ps. 66:10).
- "See, I have refined you, though not as silver; I have tested you in the furnace of affliction" (Isa. 48:10).

Your Chance to Dance:

- Make a list of current and/or past situations that were difficult or painful. Pray that God will reveal to you what He wants you to learn from them and how He wants you to grow.
- Think of someone you may comfort as a result of a difficult situation you've endured. Reach out and offer some encouragement to him or her.
- Start reading your Bible and praying daily. Watch and record how God works in your life.

Chapter Eight

REMEMBERING
GOD'S GOODNESS

*H*ow can you still find the strength to smile at your daughter's
funeral?" I'm not sure who asked the question, but I can
remember giving it a great deal of thought in the days and weeks
that followed Ashlynn's death. I cried for most of the service, but
I do remember smiling as friends and family hugged me and
expressed their sympathy. Was I emotionally and physically numb
from the pain medications (I had just had a C-section), or was
there a sense of joy in the midst of my deep sorrow? God gave us
two-and-a-half glorious days with Ashlynn. I got to see her sweet
face with her beautiful painted lips. I heard her breathe, felt her
warmth, touched her satin skin. I rubbed my cheek against hers,
stroked her soft dark hair, heard her faint cry, saw the scrunched up
face and squirms she made when she was hungry. I gave her a bath,
changed her diapers, fed her, rocked her, sang to her, and loved her.
I was her mother.

There will be no milestones to record in the baby book, no birth-
days, no first days of school, no tears over boyfriends, no wedding,
no celebration of her becoming a mother. All of my parenting of
her was wrapped into a very short time. Her memorial service was
the only gathering I'd ever plan for her. Our friends, family, church

members, and coworkers were there sharing with us. I would never be able to show her off in the grocery store or pass her around to other women at Wednesday night suppers. This was it.

In retrospect then, I think it makes sense that I showed such a wide range of emotions at the service. I was deeply saddened by her absence and missed her terribly; however, I was able to show pictures of her and share her with our family and friends as they joined us on this occasion. I also took comfort in knowing that she was now living a life in heaven that would be far better than anything I could have ever provided for her. So with mixed emotion, I found the strength to smile.

Praise and Worship

Even though God didn't heal Ashlynn, I had reason to praise Him. He gave me the opportunity to hold her and love her. Beyond that, I had to remember that He still loved me enough that He sent His Son to die on the cross so I could live in heaven for eternity with Him. According to Isaiah 61:3, Christ will provide for us a garment of praise instead of a spirit of despair, and there are endless reasons to praise and worship God. Look at the spiritual blessings we receive in Christ. We're loved, blessed, chosen, adopted, accepted, redeemed, and forgiven (Eph. 1:3–8). The God of all creation loves us and cares for us. He calls us His children.

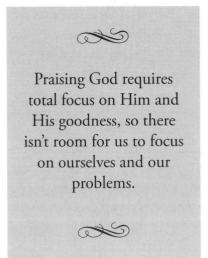

Praising God requires total focus on Him and His goodness, so there isn't room for us to focus on ourselves and our problems.

It's hard—no, it's actually impossible—to be down when you're praising God. Praising God requires total focus on Him and His goodness, so there isn't room for us to focus on ourselves and our problems. Not only is praise pleasing to God, it's a great way to improve our thoughts and attitude. He created us for worship; therefore, when we're praising Him, whether it's through prayer, music, or service, we'll experience a peace that transcends all understanding. When we're doing what we were created to do, we'll find true happiness no matter what's going on around us. Consider Psalm 103:

> Praise the LORD, O my soul; all my inmost being, praise his holy name. Praise the LORD, O my soul and forget not all his benefits—who forgives all your sins and heals all your diseases; who redeems your life from the pit and crowns you with love and compassion, who satisfies your desires with good things, so that your youth is renewed like the eagle's. The LORD works righteousness and justice for all the oppressed. He made known his ways to Moses, his deeds to the people of Israel: The LORD is compassionate and gracious, slow to anger, abounding in love. He will not always accuse, nor will he harbor his anger forever; he does not treat us as our sins deserve or repay us according to our iniquities. For as high as the heavens are above the earth, so great is his love for those who fear him; as far as the east is from the west, so far has he removed our transgressions from us. As a father has compassion on his children, so the LORD has compassion on those who fear him; for he knows how we are formed, he remembers that we are dust. As for man, his days are like grass, he flourishes like a flower of the field; the wind blows over it and it is gone, and its place remembers it no more. But from everlasting to everlasting the LORD's love is with those who fear him, and his righteousness with

their children's children—with those who keep his covenant and remember to obey his precepts. The Lord has established his throne in heaven, and his kingdom rules over all. Praise the LORD, you his angels, you mighty ones who do his bidding, who obey his word. Praise the LORD, all his heavenly hosts, you his servants who do his will. Praise the LORD, all his works everywhere in his dominion. Praise the LORD, O my soul.

Wow, what a list! He forgives, heals, and redeems. He's compassionate, gracious, slow to anger, and abounding in love, and therefore, He does not repay us as our sins deserve. And most of all, He gave His son as a sacrifice so that we might have eternal life.

What more could we possibly want? Yet how often do we find ourselves whining about our current situation? Instead, we should be remembering God for all He has done for us. This life is but a moment. We'll be in eternal bliss in the blink of an eye. Surely we can endure life's trials until then.

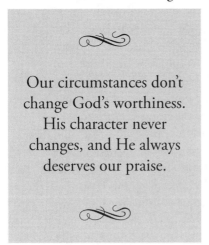

Our circumstances don't change God's worthiness. His character never changes, and He always deserves our praise.

Our circumstances don't change God's worthiness. His character never changes, and He always deserves our praise. When we're busy praising God, we're not focused on ourselves and our problems. There's immediate relief from suffering, even if only momentarily, when we're praising God. That's not to say that our issues are then solved or swept away, but over time we're able to view them from a better perspective—from a godly perspective instead of from a self-consumed viewpoint.

During my immediate grieving for Ashlynn, there were times when I just needed a break from my grief. I'm not referring to escaping the pain through unhealthy means, but instead I needed a different focus for a short time. Grieving, like many stressful situations, is physically and emotionally draining. There were times I needed to laugh or immerse myself in something else to relieve the stress of grieving. When I took those detours, my grief didn't magically disappear, but I was able to put it on hold for brief periods of time. There were times I struggled with guilt for allowing myself to laugh or do something I enjoyed. Fortunately, I was able to give myself permission to take a break because I realized I needed to stay healthy for the sake of my other children, my husband, and myself. Often times, my relief started with praising God.

We are given biblical instruction to praise God. "Praise the LORD. Praise God in his sanctuary; praise him in his mighty heavens. Praise him for his acts of power; praise him for his surpassing greatness. Praise him with the sounding of the trumpet, praise him with the harp and lyre, praise him with tambourine and dancing, praise him with the strings and flute, praise him with the clash of cymbals, praise him with resounding cymbals. Let everything that has breath praise the LORD. Praise the LORD" (Ps. 150:1–6).

There are different forms of praise, but here in Psalm 150 we clearly see the use of music. After Ashlynn's death, a friend made a compact disc of praise songs for me and I listened to it repeatedly. Eventually, God's promises that were conveyed in the lyrics sunk into my being and I found that I was singing the songs. Over time, my singing praise songs progressed to praising God through prayer and other expressions. And the more I praised Him, the better I felt. My thoughts became clear and focused. I felt that I was emerging from the darkness.

Praising Him took the focus off of my pain and helped me turn to God. He truly is worthy of our praise.

Paul and Silas are great examples of people praising God in spite of pain and suffering. In Acts 16, Paul and Silas were seized, beaten, and thrown into prison. Yet, in the middle of the night, they were praying and singing hymns of praise to God. They were able to rejoice in Christ in spite of their persecution. They were truly filled with the Spirit and able to see beyond their circumstances.

Paul's attitude is summarized in several verses in another one of his letters. "Therefore we do not lose heart, but though our outer man is decaying, yet our inner man is being renewed day by day. For momentary, light affliction is producing for us an eternal weight of glory far beyond all comparison" (2 Cor. 4:16–17 NASB). Later he shares Christ's words, "My grace is sufficient for you, for power is perfected in weakness," and adds, "Most gladly, therefore, I will rather boast about my weaknesses, so that the power of Christ may dwell in me. Therefore I am well content with weaknesses, with insults, with distresses, with persecutions, with difficulties, for Christ's sake; for when I am weak, then I am strong" (2 Cor. 12:9–10 NASB).

Always Give Thanks

Praising God should be taken a step further. "Give thanks to the LORD, call on his name; make known among the nations what he has done. Sing to him, sing praise to him; tell of all his wonderful acts. Glory in his holy name; let the hearts of those who seek the LORD rejoice. Look to the LORD and his strength; seek his face always. Remember the wonders he has done, his miracles, and the judgments he pronounced" (Ps. 105:1–5). These verses reflect activity. Not only are we to remember God's goodness, we're to go out and tell about it. In doing so, we take the focus off of our trials and give God glory.

No matter what may be going on in my life, I try to always find something for which I'm thankful. After Ashlynn died, there were days when it was very hard to think of even one thing to be thankful for because I was so consumed by grief; however, when I could find one thing—even if it was simply to say, "Thank you God for the beautiful flowers you created"—I would begin to feel better. Somehow, my cluttered, overwhelming thoughts were cleared and I could regain my focus on Him.

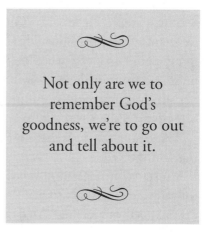

Not only are we to remember God's goodness, we're to go out and tell about it.

The process was slow, but each day I was able to find more and more things for which to give thanks. And the more thankful I was, the more I was able to praise God. The cycle began a positive upward climb towards restoration. First Thessalonians 5:16–18 became verses of mediation and reflection for me. It says, "Be joyful always; pray continually; give thanks in all circumstances, for this is God's will for you in Christ Jesus." The more I prayed and the more I thanked God, the more joyful my spirit became.

We're given more instruction in Philippians 4:4–7. "Rejoice in the Lord always. I will say it again: Rejoice! Let your gentleness be evident to all. The Lord is near. Do not be anxious about anything, but in everything, by prayer and petition, with thanksgiving, present your requests to God. And the peace of God, which transcends all understanding, will guard your hearts and your minds in Christ Jesus." Again we see that praise and a heart of thanksgiving lead to peace. Although it seems counterintuitive, try thanking God during trying times. You'll likely be amazed by the results.

When the Answer Is "No"

There was silence the moment Ashlynn was born. She was a bluish color and made no sound. I was holding my breath. Seconds later, a nurse said, "Quick, you can touch her before we examine her." I still couldn't hear anything. I could just see in my peripheral view what looked like a flurry of activity. Still no sound from Ashlynn. They brought her back to me and laid her on my chest. Still no sound. Finally, I asked the dreaded question, "Is she alive?"

"Yes," came the answer from the nurse. "She's barely breathing, but she's alive."

As I stared at Ashlynn, I was dumbfounded. Finally the doctor said, "You can talk to her."

I snapped out of my dazed state and began talking to her lovingly. As I did, she started to breathe at a near normal rate. What a relief! Almost immediately, though, panic set in. I wanted my other two daughters to see their sister alive, and it appeared that time was critical. It was clear that Ashlynn was not well and we weren't sure how much time we would have with her.

> God chose to tell me "no" to my ultimate desire, so I was faced with a choice about what and how I thought about God.

When I first learned of Ashlynn's condition early in the pregnancy, my very first prayer was, "God, please let me hold her alive." As time passed, I became bolder in my request and asked God to heal her; however, God chose to tell me "no" to my ultimate desire, so I was faced with a choice about what and how I thought about God. Would I continue to love Him for who He is or

120

was my love for Him based solely on what He does? Ultimately, I had to trust Him. God tells us in Jeremiah 29:11, "'For I know the plans I have for you,' declares the LORD, 'plans to prosper you and not to harm you, plans to give you hope and a future.'" But how could that be? How could the death of my child be part of His plan?

Are you struggling with similar questions? What hardship in your life doesn't make sense? Is it divorce or the loss of a job? Is it the loss of a loved one, your own failing health, or something else? We may never understand why some things happen, but as children of God we need to remember that He loves us.

If you're a parent you may have an understanding of this concept. Our children often don't understand our decisions, partly because they don't have the capacity to understand and partly because we sometimes don't provide them with all the necessary information to understand. Our heavenly Father is similar to the parent in this scenario. Isaiah 55:8 says, "'For my thoughts are not your thoughts, neither are your ways my ways,' declares the LORD." As hard as it may be to submit to God's plan, the truth is that it's the first step to acceptance. Trusting Him and His plan is integral to experiencing emotional healing.

I've accepted God's will for Ashlynn's life and I've come to know Him deeper through my journey. I trust that He wants good things for me. I believe that He loves me. As a result, I've continued to share my desires and present my requests to Him. Not only have I asked him to show me the good in my circumstances, but I've asked for comfort, healing, encouragement, and reminders of His presence. I've even asked Him at various times to help me remember Ashlynn in new and different ways, and He's answered in surprising revelations at just the right times.

As time passed, I found myself longing for a real reminder of how Ashlynn's skin felt. I couldn't find anything around me that compared to the delicate, soft skin that encapsulated her tiny body. So, with great expectation, I began to pray that God would show me something tangible that was comparable to the feel of her skin. I remember the moment I made the discovery. It was so simple and obvious. How could I have missed it? But in God's way and timing, the moment of discovery became a precious gift and an expression of His love. I was taking a short retreat to the local botanical gardens. I desperately needed some quiet time—time to reflect, time to reenergize. As I sat there on the perfect autumn day, I would gaze at the beautiful landscape around me. I would spend quiet time in prayer and alternately look up to appreciate the beauty. It was a warm sunny day with a gentle breeze that carried the scent of roses. I could feel the warmth of the sun on my skin and was calm and relaxed. As I sat in the midst of the rose garden, I leaned over to touch one of the petals. A simple white rose, delicate, petite, and the feel of Ashlynn's skin. The setting and mood was ideal for the wondrous discovery. And, it was all perfectly orchestrated by the hand of God.

Another time, I started praying that God would give me a glimpse of what Ashlynn is doing. I wasn't sure what to expect, but I waited with hope and anticipation. Some time later I was riding with my middle daughter in a convertible and enjoying the countryside. She has no real memories of her baby sister because she was so young when Ashlynn was born; however, she sometimes talks about her being in heaven. We were riding quietly enjoying the beautiful day and the wind in our hair when she suddenly broke the silence. "Momma, I hear Ashlynn laughing in my heart." Stunned, all that formed on my lips was the question, "You do?" She said, "Yes, Jesus is tickling her." Tears pooled in my eyes as I thought of such a playful and endearing image. I'm certain Jesus is loving on her and she's enjoying her home in heaven. I may never know what prompted my daughter's words that day, but I trust that the message was intended for me.

God's love for me is evident in very real and practical ways. So, even though He didn't answer in the affirmative and spare Ashlynn's life, I trust He has a good plan. I encourage you to love Him for who He is, not whether He always gives you what you want. Remember, God is always good.

God Says:

- "How great is your goodness, which you have stored up for those who fear you, which you bestow in the sight of men on those who take refuge in you" (Ps. 31:19).
- "Devote yourselves to prayer, being watchful and thankful" (Col. 4:2).
- "Give thanks to the LORD, call on his name; make known among the nations what he has done" (1 Chron. 16:8).
- "Give thanks to the Lord, for he is good; his love endures forever" (1 Chron. 16:34).
- "They were also to stand every morning to thank and praise the Lord. They were to do the same in the evening" (1 Chron. 23:30).
- "I will give thanks to the LORD because of his righteousness and will sing praise to the name of the LORD Most High" (Ps. 7:17).
- "The LORD is my strength and my shield; my heart trusts in him, and I am helped. My heart leaps for joy and I will give thanks to him in song" (Ps. 28:7).
- "That my heart may sing to you and not be silent. O LORD my God, I will give you thanks forever" (Ps. 30:12).
- "Enter his gates with thanksgiving and his courts with praise; give thanks to him and praise his name" (Ps. 100:4).
- "Praise the LORD. Give thanks to the LORD, for he is good; his love endures forever" (Ps. 106:1).
- "Let them give thanks to the LORD for his unfailing love and his wonderful deeds for men" (Ps. 107:8).

- "I will give you thanks, for you answered me; you have become my salvation" (Ps. 118:21).
- "You are my God, and I will give you thanks; you are my God, and I will exalt you" (Ps. 118:28).
- "From the rising of the sun to the place where it sets, the name of the LORD is to be praised" (Ps. 113:3).
- "I praise you because I am fearfully and wonderfully made; your works are wonderful, I know that full well" (Ps. 139:14).
- "Great is the LORD and most worthy of praise; his greatness no one can fathom" (Ps. 145:3).

Your Chance to Dance:

- Begin every day with a prayer of thanksgiving.
- Keep a prayer journal. Record prayer requests and how God answers. Periodically review it to see evidence of His goodness.
- Carry or keep a rock of remembrance. Keep a stone in your jacket pocket or place a special rock in a flower garden to remind you of what God has done for you.
- Create a basket of thanksgiving. As good things happen, record them on a note card and place the card in a designated box or basket. Periodically read through the cards to be reminded of God's blessings and goodness in your life.
- Read a chapter in the book of Psalms daily.

Chapter Nine

REAPING A HARVEST

*W*hile *pregnant with Ashlynn, I had the opportunity to assist a lady with a young child in the parking lot of the grocery store. She had inadvertently locked her keys in her car as she was putting her groceries in the trunk. As she stood there frantically trying to figure out what to do, I said a prayer and then approached her to offer my help. She had borrowed a cell phone from someone else, but wasn't able to reach her husband. We looked around her car and noticed that she'd left her front window open just a little. That was just enough room for me to stick my small umbrella into her car and release the lock on her door. She was ecstatic. She jumped up and down and hugged me. As I returned to my car, she yelled, "Your blessings will come!"*

Her comment stuck with me for several weeks. I'd replay the words in the mind over and over. *Your blessings will come.* I'd wonder what form that blessing would take, but I was often thinking in concrete, temporal ways. I wasn't thinking eternally. The reality is that we often want earthly blessings. We may even judge our success by such blessings; however, once again, we should turn our focus toward heaven.

Sowing Seed

We've all heard the saying, "You reap what you sow." There's a lot of truth in that statement, but let's explore it a little deeper. Begin thinking about all that's involved in the growing cycle of a garden. First you have to prepare the soil—turning it, removing weeds and rocks, and adding necessary compost material to enhance its quality. Then you must make mounds or rows for sowing the seed. The seeds need to be carefully sifted to remove unhealthy ones and then soaked in preparation for planting. Finally, they are placed at the appropriate depth in the soil, covered, and watered. If all goes well and they get the appropriate amount of water and sunlight, you'll have something edible in a couple of months. Also consider that during that time, the plants must be tended. There's fertilizing, staking, weeding, supplemental watering, and more weeding. A lot of work goes into growing that precious fruit or vegetable before finally enjoying the harvested product. There's only one guarantee in the whole process—if you planted green bean seeds, you'll harvest green beans, not tomatoes, or carrots, or peppers.

Likewise, think about what we sow on a daily basis. Are we sowing seeds of kindness, goodness, and love even though life is tough? Are we serving others when we really want to be the recipient of those acts of service? Are we speaking words of encouragement even when we've been hurt?

God assures us that the harvest is sweet if we work at it until the right time.

I'll admit that it's hard to do the right thing. We're human, and we have to battle our flesh. Our nature is to focus on ourselves and choose things that are most comfortable, even pleasurable. Included in that is our struggle with delayed gratification. We want our reward now. But just like the fruit that's produced from an apple seed, it takes time to experience the harvest. However, God assures us that the harvest is sweet if we work at it until the right time.

Eternal Rewards

God's Word tells us that we will be rewarded for seeking Him and serving Him. The Bible tells us we'll encounter heartbreak and hardships, but we'll be rewarded in heaven for seeking the will of God and offering ourselves fully to Him even in the midst of suffering. As committed believers we'll be persecuted, but God's reward will be far greater than any suffering we will experience here on earth. At the end, we should be able to say as Paul said to Timothy in 2 Timothy 4:7, "I have fought the good fight, I have finished the race, I have kept the faith."

As believers, we are co-heirs with Christ (Rom. 8:17) and we're told in Revelation 3:21, "To him who overcomes, I will give the right to sit with me on my throne, just as I overcame and sat down with my Father on his throne." James 1:12 states, "Blessed is the man who perseveres under trial, because when he has stood the test, he will receive the crown of life that God has promised to those who love him." The crown of life is our ultimate reward—our eternal life in heaven. We're also told in the Gospels that Jesus has gone ahead of us and has prepared many mansions for us in heaven. So the journey may be tough, but the reward is great. Can you even imagine what it means to be a co-heir with Christ? My mind can hardly comprehend that God loves us that much.

Earthly Rewards

God has a track record of bestowing earthly rewards, and He does so in many forms. Although our tendency may be to think of blessings as material possessions, there are some earthly rewards that are far greater than wealth, including the experience of His presence, the revelation of His will to us, and the experience of His peace and love. Let's explore some of God's blessings based on examples from the Bible.

The Old Testament book of Isaiah says that God's people will receive a double portion instead of shame and disgrace and that everlasting joy will be theirs (Isa. 61:7). Notice that God didn't just bless His people, but He gave abundantly. We can be assured that God has great things in store for those who endure hardship, especially when we glorify Him in the process. He promises to bestow a crown of beauty on His children instead of ashes, the oil of gladness instead of mourning, and a garment of praise instead of despair (Isa. 61:3). These promises refer to earthly blessings. These blessings may come in our attitude and thoughts instead of as worldly possessions, but

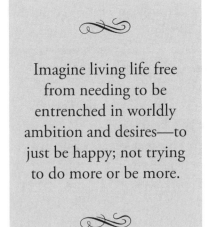

Imagine living life free from needing to be entrenched in worldly ambition and desires—to just be happy; not trying to do more or be more.

we're encouraged again that we can experience joy whatever life brings . . . and what a gift it is—peace, joy, and gladness. This is life at its best. Imagine living life free from needing to be entrenched in worldly ambition and desires—to just be happy; not trying to do more or be more.

There is also the reward of experiencing God—being in His very presence. You may be familiar with the story of Shadrach, Meshach, and Abednego in the book of Daniel. King Nebuchadnezzar ordered that all the people of the land were to worship his gods and the gold idol he had created. When he received word that Shadrach, Meshach, and Abednego were disobeying his rule, he summoned them and warned of the punishment for disobedience. They replied, "O Nebuchadnezzar, we do not need to defend ourselves before you in this matter. If we are thrown into the blazing furnace, the God we serve is able to save us from it, and he will rescue us from your hand, O king. But even if he does not, we want you to know, O king, that we will not serve your gods or worship the image of gold you have set up" (Dan. 3:16–18). They did not try to lie or talk their way out of the "offense." They remained true to God even though it had serious consequences. Notice that they believed God's ability to save them, but they acknowledged that He may not choose to do so. Nonetheless, they remained faithful. There's no mention of them even complaining or questioning God about their circumstances. And the result is that an angel of the Lord appeared with them in the fiery furnace and they were delivered unscathed. They witnessed a miracle, experienced God's presence, and the glory of God was revealed to all those who saw and heard.

The life of Ruth is another great example. When her husband died, she chose to stay with her mother-in-law, Naomi, instead of returning to her homeland. This was a significant act of love for several reasons. First, she was a Moabite by descent and was raised to worship false gods. Instead of returning to her family, she chose to stay with Naomi and recognize God as the true God. She chose to worship Him. Secondly, being a young widow with no children, she had no future and no means to sustain herself for the present, either. Yet, she stayed with Naomi and returned to Bethlehem. God honored her decisions by pouring out many blessings on her. She went from poverty to marrying a wealthy farmer named Boaz. They gave birth to a son, and she later became the great-grandmother of King David, making her part of the lineage of Jesus. Those are some pretty amazing blessings!

Later, we see blessings in the life of Job for his loyalty to God. He experienced the loss of wealth, children, and health, yet he remained faithful to the Lord. He even experienced the criticism of his friends during his trials, who suggested the things that happened to him were a result of his sin. All the while, Job continued to love the Lord. In the end, the Lord made him prosperous again and gave him twice as much as he had before (Job 42:10).

In the book of Deuteronomy, the rewards of obedience and the curse of disobedience are clearly described. His blessings are tangible. The Bible says that the Lord will "open the heavens, the storehouse of his bounty" (Deut. 28:12). But again, it specifically states these blessings are for obedience. Are we acting in obedience and following the guidelines God gives? Are we compassionate and forgiving? Do we guard our mouths from gossip and our minds from worry? Do we place greater emphasis on carrying out God's work instead of our own agendas?

Obviously we fall short of God's commands. We are imperfect humans. However, what is the true condition of our hearts? God knows the answer, and I believe that God blesses our efforts to follow His Word even when we miss the mark. I think about my daughters' abilities to make their beds. There is a big difference in abilities, with my oldest daughter being three years her sister's senior. Because of their age difference, my expectations for them are different. If my oldest daughter makes a half-hearted attempt to make her bed, it looks about the same as when my younger daughter makes her best effort. Do I reprimand my younger daughter for not being as skilled as her sister? No. Instead, I praise her effort and recognize that the more she practices the better she'll be able to accomplish the task. It boils down to attitude. I reward their best efforts, not the final product or result of their performance. I think God views us in a similar way.

God's plans are for abundance and prosperity. In Jeremiah it says, "'For I know the plans I have for you,' declares the LORD, 'plans to prosper you and not to harm you, plans to give you hope and a future. Then you will call upon me and come and pray to me, and I will listen to you. You will seek me and find me when you seek me with all your heart. I will be found by you,' declares the LORD, 'and will bring you back from captivity'" (Jer. 19:11–14).

God will rescue from captivity. He wants us to be free. And although He sometimes uses challenging situations to grab our attention, the freedom that results from a close relationship with Him is sweetness to the soul.

God wants us to experience His fullness in life. Peace, joy, love—to a full measure. Instead of Satan's desire for us—oppression and destruction—God tells us that He sent Jesus so we could live a life of abundance.

Jesus told the parable of the talents, which focuses on the consequences of the choices we make. In this story, the master gives his servants talents (a form of money worth more than a thousand dollars) according to each person's abilities. One received five talents, one received two talents and the final servant received one. The master then began a journey and entrusted each of the servants to the property he had left them. Note that He didn't give everyone the same amount, yet He trusted each with something. I make this point because how often are we tempted to compare our lives—even our possessions—to those of others? We are tempted to fall into the trap of thinking that others have been blessed with greater

God wants us to experience His fullness in life.

abundance and thinking it's unfair. Do you think your home is smaller and less beautiful than your friends' homes? Or do you ever wonder why God blessed you with one child instead of two or three or more? It's important that we stay focused on using our skills and resources to the best of our ability in serving God. So if our home isn't as big and beautiful as others, we should still take care of it to the best of our ability and use it to be a blessing to others and a place where others will experience the love of God. If you only have one child, be the best parent you can be and train them up in the love of God. Perhaps you'd rather be a leader than a server. God deems each role as equally important. Both are needed for the body of Christ to function in unity. So when you serve, do it to the best of your ability. Thank God for what He's given you. See your gifts and blessings as exactly that—gifts and blessings—and use them to glorify Him.

As the parable of the talents continues, we learn that the first two servants went to work immediately and were able to double their money using their skills and abilities. However, the third servant decided to bury his money in the ground until the master returned. Upon his return, the master was pleased that the first two men had each doubled what was entrusted to them. He was equally pleased with their efforts even though one had earned more than the other, because they had each worked according to their own God-given abilities. However, He went on to call the third servant lazy and wicked and took the one talent and gave it to the servant with ten talents. He closes by saying that everyone who has will be given more, and he will have an abundance (Matt. 25:29).

There are several lessons to be learned in this parable, but I use it here as an example of God's blessing on those who are obedient to Him. His gives us our talents, abilities, and even financial resources so we can promote His kingdom, not for personal gain. When we use our gifts in ways that glorify Him, He blesses us with more. He wants to pour out His blessings on us so we can be an outpouring of His love and blessing to others.

I can remember traveling with a group of friends following high school graduation. There were several carloads of us traveling in a caravan. Unbeknownst to me, as we went through a toll plaza, the driver of the car in front of me paid his toll as well as mine. The unexpected gesture of kindness surprised me and I simply said, "Thank you," to the attendant and commented to my passengers that it was a thoughtful act. However, what I should have done was to pass along the favor to the group behind me so the kindness could have been communicated through our entire group.

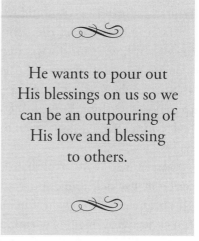

He wants to pour out His blessings on us so we can be an outpouring of His love and blessing to others.

The incident makes me wonder how many opportunities I have missed to be an instrument of God and a blessing to others. Perhaps I was "too busy" to let go of my agenda. Or maybe I was consumed by the task at hand. Or, dare I say it? I was too focused on myself to see the opportunity. How many times has God blessed me, and instead of sharing it with others I gratefully accept, end of story? In the busyness of life it's easy to get caught up in just doing what I need to do and become forgetful of my calling to help others. I have started looking for ways to bless others, even asking God to bring ideas and people to mind. And what a joy it is! It lifts my spirits and hopefully spreads some love and joy.

Surprises

I love surprises. I like to surprise other people, and I enjoy it when I'm surprised by an unexpected gesture of kindness or love. I believe that God also likes surprises. My daughter often asks what heaven will be like. I do my best to explain it to her as I understand it from Scripture; however, I always end by telling her there will be lots of wonderful surprises. She takes great delight in this as should we.

I believe that one of the surprises in heaven will be perfect understanding. Our lives often appear like the back of a tapestry—a blended mess of color and texture. We often aren't able to see how all the broken pieces of our lives fit together to make something beautiful. However, in heaven we'll finally reach our perfected state. Then the beautiful side of the tapestry will be revealed.

Heaven is so wonderful that there aren't human words to describe it. Ezekiel, John, and Paul did their best to describe the glimpses they were given, but the Bible concedes that no one can conceive or imagine what God has in store for us. Knowing that we serve an amazing God, I trust that heaven will be incredible, and I look forward to spending eternity there.

We need to stand strong in our beliefs and hold tight to God during tough times. The rewards are amazing—both now and for eternity—for our faithfulness, obedience, and service to Christ. I trust with all my being that I won't be disappointed.

God Says:

- "Let us not become weary in doing good, for at the proper time we will reap a harvest if we do not give up" (Gal. 6:9).
- "Surely you have granted him eternal blessings and made him glad with the joy of your presence" (Ps. 21:6).

- "Blessed are all who fear the LORD, who walk in his ways. You will eat the fruit of your labor; blessings and prosperity will be yours" (Ps. 128:1–2).
- "Those who sow in tears will reap with songs of joy. He who goes out weeping, carrying seed to sow, will return with songs of joy" (Ps. 126:5–6).
- "May the peoples praise you, O God; may all the peoples praise you. Then the land will yield its harvest, and God, our God, will bless us" (Ps. 67:5–6).
- "The Lord will indeed give what is good, and our land will yield its harvest" (Ps. 85:12).
- "Blessings crown the head of the righteous" (Prov. 10:6).
- "You, O Lord, are loving. Surely you will reward each person according to what he has done" (Ps. 62:12).
- "He who is kind to the poor lends to the LORD, and he will reward him for what he has done" (Prov. 19:17).
- "If your enemy is hungry, give him food to eat; if he is thirsty, give him water to drink. In doing this, you will heap burning coals on his head, and the LORD will reward you" (Prov. 25:21–22).
- "Blessed are you when people insult you, persecute you and falsely say all kinds of evil against you because of me. Rejoice and be glad, because great is your reward in heaven, for in the same way they persecuted the prophets who were before you" (Matt. 5:11–12).
- "For the Son of Man is going to come in his Father's glory with his angels, and then he will reward each person according to what he has done" (Matt. 16:27).
- "Whatever you do, work at it with all your heart, as working for the Lord, not for men, since you know that you will receive an inheritance from the Lord as a reward. It is the Lord Christ you are serving" (Col. 3:23–24).
- "Who, then, is the man that fears the LORD? He will instruct him in the way chosen for him. He will spend

his days in prosperity, and his descendants will inherit the land" (Ps. 25:12–13).

- "The thief comes only to steal and kill and destroy; I have come that they may have life, and have it to the full" (John 10:10).

Your Chance to Dance:

- Make a list of your most valued treasures. Are they mostly earthly things or things with eternal value? How can you ensure that your focus remains on God?
- Ask God to show you ways that you can serve Him on a daily basis.
- What are some godly characteristics you would like to harvest? List practical ways to sow those traits in your daily life. (For example, if you would like to be a patient person, list practical and specific ways—including prayer—of how you can respond with patience in challenging circumstances.)
- Seek God daily through Bible study and prayer. Select a weekly Bible verse to memorize and meditate on throughout each day.

Chapter Ten

THE CHOICE

*I*t continues to bewilder me that I was given the choice of ending *Ashlynn's life. I can't imagine my life without having known her. Even more confusing to me is the response of those around me who somehow thought my decision to carry her to term reflected strength. In my mind, ending her life wasn't an option, so it really wasn't a choice at all; however, how I live my life is a choice. Will I strive to live as Christ wants me to live and tell of His goodness? This is the real choice for each of us.*

Bitter or Better

We probably all know someone who has chosen to be bitter about life instead of making the most of things. You know the person who is critical about almost everyone and everything. She never seems happy in life and rarely has anything positive to say. Hopefully you're not one of those people, but if you are, there's hope!

Bitterness is essentially anger and disappointment that have never been resolved. Bitterness can build over time and escalate to gargantuan proportions. That's exactly what Satan wants from you and me. He wants us buried under a mountain of frustration and unhappiness that makes us ineffective followers of Christ. Think about it. If we're so consumed by our circumstances, we won't have time to focus on sharing God's love with others. We may give dutifully of our time and resources to the church, but our everyday life is a not a reflection of Christ's love. What a sad existence!

(Satan) wants us buried under a mountain of frustration and unhappiness that makes us ineffective followers of Christ.

We Christians are filled with the Holy Spirit and should therefore demonstrate the fruit of the Spirit—love, joy, peace, patience, kindness, goodness, faithfulness, gentleness, and self-control. Would you rather be angry and irritated most of your life or learn from your circumstances and choose to be happy?

George Mueller, an English evangelist and philanthropist in the 1800s, once said, "The greater the trial, the sweeter the victory."[1] That's the right attitude for success. He was able to see that even though life may not be fair, it pays to persevere, especially when the Lord is involved. All things are possible through Christ who strengthens us. Our actions and attitudes reflect whether or not we truly believe this promise.

I'm not sure what makes people choose different routes when faced with the critical decision of how to respond to hardships. I'm sure there are a hundred psychology theories that attempt to explain it. An entire field of study on resiliency exists. According to resiliencycenter.com, resiliency is "a human ability to recover from disruptive change or misfortune without being overwhelmed or acting in dysfunctional or harmful ways."[2] We each possess varying degrees of qualities that facilitate resiliency. Some of those qualities include:

- Emotional awareness—understands and identifies feelings
- Perseverance—doesn't give up
- Internal locus of control—motivates self instead of reliance on external forces
- Optimism—sees the positive in most situations
- Support—surrounds oneself with supportive friends and family
- Sense of humor—able to laugh at life's difficulties
- Perspective—finds meaning in life's challenges
- Spirituality—especially if internally connected, not just going through the motions of attending services[3]

Although there are many helpful characteristics listed, I suggest that spirituality is the most important quality. If Jesus is my rock and refuge, then I have a strong foundation. If I'm centered on Him, then I'll be upheld by His promises. There's hope in knowing that my suffering isn't without purpose or gain.

In the midst of our crisis, our goal may simply be survival. At some point though, we must take a step towards healing. Ashlynn's death was a defining moment, and I was forever changed. I had to make sense of who I had become and what would become my new "normal." Everything in my world had changed because of one event, and nothing seemed to fit anymore. My desire was and is to become better instead of bitter.

Bloom Where You're Planted

There comes a point of realization in our suffering when we have to face the reality that we can't go back to the way things used to be. Whatever the crisis, life is now different and no matter how bad we wish we could go back, we can't. We're faced with a decision. We can accept our new reality and move on, or we can expend all of our energy being disappointed that things are now different. Obviously there's a time of transition when we grieve the loss, but eventually we need to find meaning in life as it now exists.

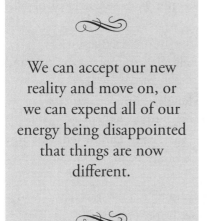

We can accept our new reality and move on, or we can expend all of our energy being disappointed that things are now different.

In my situation, I had to realize that God still had a purpose and plan for me—possibly bigger than I could imagine. Ashlynn's life and death had significant meaning, and God had a purpose for choosing me to be her mother. I want to learn from that. Not only does it give my life greater meaning to seek God's purpose for my new reality, but it gives meaning to my daughter's brief existence. I get great comfort knowing that she fulfilled God's calling for her life. Ultimately, I want to know that my suffering was not in vain, but that it served some greater purpose.

After learning of Ashlynn's prognosis, it would have been easy to mourn for the remainder of the pregnancy. I don't think anyone would have blamed me for choosing to do so, but I would have been miserable the entire time and missed many opportunities to enjoy her life and praise God. Instead, I chose to savor every moment because I didn't know how long I'd have with her.

Since a traditional baby shower was not appropriate, we decided to have a "celebration of life" gathering. Friends and family gathered and brought Scripture, poems, prayers, and messages to share. The time was special and the gathering gave me the opportunity to share her with others while recognizing her for the special and important life that she was. She was still one of my children and I wanted to honor her. Had I been moping around, I would have missed a wonderful opportunity to celebrate her precious life.

We're in control of how we respond to our circumstances. We may not be able to control the situation itself, but we can choose how we behave and react. Do you want to choose the path of learning and growth or the path of bitterness and destruction? Although it may be easier to react in accordance with our feelings, it's well worth the effort to step back and try a godly approach. God tells His people, "Those who hope in me will not be disappointed" (Isa. 49:23). Are you willing to trust Him?

Charles Swindoll says this about attitude:

> The longer I live, the more I realize the impact of attitude on life. Attitude, to me, is more important than facts. It is more important than the past, than education, than money, than circumstances, than failures, than successes, than what other people think, say or do. It is more important than appearance, giftedness or skill. It will make or break a company . . . a church . . . a home. The remarkable thing is we have a choice every day regarding the attitude we embrace for that day. We cannot change our past . . . we cannot change the fact that people will act in a certain way. We cannot change the inevitable. The only thing we can do is play the one

string we have, and that is our attitude . . . I am
convinced that life is 10% what happens to me and
90% how I react to it. And so it is with you . . . we
are in charge of our attitudes.[4]

There was a time when my husband battled a tendency to
be negative. He was even nicknamed "Eeyore" by a group of
friends in college because of this tendency. He eventually made
a conscious effort to be more positive, encouraging, and upbeat,
but during especially busy or stressful times, he would revert
back to his previous ways in the safety of home. Unfortunately,
that meant that we saw the less attractive side of his personality.
As old habits emerged and lingered, I became resentful. I also
found that I was becoming more negative. And of course, he
was an easy target to blame. It was, after all, *his* negativity that
was the cause of mine.

Although it took a while, I began to realize that this was a
false assumption and that I didn't need to react to his negativity. I was participating in a Bible study about being a godly wife
and God's perspective became very clear to me. I am account-
able to God for my own thoughts and actions; my husband
must answer for himself. I decided that I wasn't going to let his
behavior rob me of my happiness. I started to pray about my
attitude and ability to stay focused on God instead of my sur-
roundings. I prayed that I would view my husband as a child of
God, focus on his many good traits, and that I would exhibit an
extra measure of compassion toward him. Finally, I prayed that
if God wasn't going to deliver me from being on the receiving
end of my husband's negative ways, that He would give me the
strength to endure it.

God has been faithful in answering my prayer. He has given
me the patience and strength I've needed as I've tapped into
Him and His power. He has also given my husband successful
strides in overcoming his struggle with his negative attitude

and behavior. But along the way, the moment I'd take my eyes off Christ, I would start to feel sorry for myself again and get grumpy and demanding of my so-called rights.

I've discovered that if I want to be fruitful—which brings true happiness—then I need to stay focused on God and not my circumstances. God truly is bigger than any giant I may face—fear, boredom, busyness, loneliness, depression, poor health, and so on—and my joy can only be complete as I earnestly seek Him.

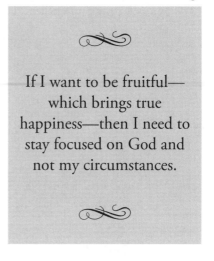

If I want to be fruitful—which brings true happiness—then I need to stay focused on God and not my circumstances.

We are assured that no matter the circumstances, we can't be torn from God's loving arms and character.

> Who shall separate us from the love of Christ? Shall trouble or hardship or persecution or famine or nakedness or danger or sword? As it is written: "For your sake we face death all day long; we are considered as sheep to be slaughtered." No, in all these things we are more than conquerors through him who loved us. For I am convinced that neither death nor life, neither angels nor demons, neither the present nor the future, nor any powers, neither height nor depth, nor anything else in all creation, will be able to separate us from the love of God that is in Christ Jesus our Lord.
>
> (Romans 8:35–39)

However, to fully experience His love requires a choice. It requires faith, and it requires guarding our hearts and minds, especially during the tough times. Otherwise, Satan will take any opportunity to try to convince us that our entire existence is hard and miserable.

God recently blessed our family with another child, a son. I have so much for which to be thankful; however, in the midst of sleepless nights and endless days of diapers, feedings, reflux,

To fully experience His love requires a choice. It requires faith, and it requires guarding our hearts and minds, especially during the tough times.

and laundry, I found myself longing to escape the drudgery. I caught myself dreaming of when my son is older and self-sufficient, when life will be easy again.

Then I realized how negative my thoughts were. The reality is that these are special times with my son and I should want to enjoy them. This realization helped me change my attitude even though my circumstances stayed the same. He will be little for such a short time and I don't want to miss this time or wish it away. I want to enjoy his sweet little cry as a young infant before that sound becomes the ear-piercing screams of a toddler. I want to enjoy the stillness of night with him snuggled close before he pushes me away because he's a "big boy." I want to view the laundry, cleaning, diapering, and feeding as a ministry and calling instead of a chore.

My children are a blessing, and my roles as wife and mother are a gift from God. When I do my work as if doing it for the Lord, it suddenly becomes a lighter load because it has meaning and purpose. God has given me this time in my life to care for my children and family and I want to savor it.

Even at such a glorious time in my life, I began to complain. It's even easier to complain when strife and tragedy strike. I urge you to stand strong in Jesus when the hard times come. Whatever storm is around you, let God be the source of calm within. You can endure the trial if you're close to Him. He's ready and waiting for you to allow Him to handle things for you.

Jesus tells us in John 10:10 that He came so we could have a life of abundance. The Greek meaning of the word *abundance* used in the text includes superior, extraordinary, surpassing, and uncommon. Jesus didn't come so we could be miserable or even just live common, ordinary lives. He wants us overflowing with His joy so that His love is visible to the world. He wants us so full of His Spirit that we are victorious in all that we do and that His glory is revealed.

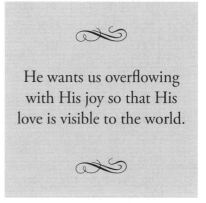

He wants us overflowing with His joy so that His love is visible to the world.

We are reminded in Hebrews that Jesus is able to sympathize with all our weaknesses because He, too, was tempted in every way. We're told, "Let us then approach the throne of grace with confidence, so that we may receive mercy and find grace to help us in our time of need" (Heb. 4:16). God is offering His mercy and grace in your time of need. Will you accept His gifts? Will you receive His love and goodness?

As we draw near the end of our journey together, I'll share one final story. In the late 1800s, a man name Horatio Spafford was inspired to write a powerful hymn that has been passed along through the ages. This hymn was written after several traumatic events in Spafford's life. His only son died in 1871, and shortly thereafter, he experienced financial ruin from the great Chicago fire. A couple of years later, he had planned to travel to Europe with his family, but sent the family ahead while he was delayed on business. While sailing across the Atlantic, the ship carrying his remaining family sank after a collision with another vessel. All four of Spafford's daughters died; only his wife survived. As he traveled to meet his grief-stricken wife, he was inspired to write these words:

> When peace like a river attendeth my way,
> When sorrows like sea billows roll;
> Whatever my lot, Thou hast taught me to say,
> It is well, it is well, with my soul.
> It is well with my soul,
> It is well, it is well, with my soul.
> Though Satan should buffet, though trials should come,
> Let this blest assurance control,
> That Christ has regarded my helpless estate,
> And hath shed His own blood for my soul.
> My sin, oh, the bliss of this glorious thought!
> My sin, not in part but the whole,
> Is nailed to the cross, and I bear it no more,
> Praise the Lord, praise the Lord, O my soul!
> And Lord, haste the day when my faith shall be sight,
> The clouds be rolled back as a scroll;
> The trump shall resound, and the Lord shall descend,
> Even so, it is well with my soul.[5]

Dear friend, are you able to say "It is well with my soul," whatever comes your way? The choice is yours. You can wallow in your sorrow or you can stand up and dance in the rain. Although it requires a lot of work to get up and dance, God will honor your choice and you'll reclaim the joy you're longing for. You will also bring great glory to Him in the process. My prayer is that you will experience God in a mighty and powerful new way and that you come to know Him as Father and

Friend. He's waiting with open arms. Grace and blessings to you as you choose to dance.

God Says:

- "And we know that in all things God works for the good of those who love him, who have been called according to his purpose" (Rom. 8:28).
- "But the eyes of the Lord are on those who fear him, on those whose hope is in his unfailing love" (Ps. 33:18).
- "We wait in hope for the Lord; he is our help and our shield" (Ps. 33:20).
- "I will praise you forever for what you have done; in your name I will hope, for your name is good. I will praise you in the presence of your saints" (Ps. 52:9).
- "Find rest, O my soul, in God alone; my hope comes from him" (Ps. 62:5).
- "O Israel, put your hope in the Lord, for with the Lord is unfailing love and with him is full redemption" (Ps. 130:7).
- "The Lord delights in those who fear him, who put their hope in his unfailing love" (Ps. 147:11).
- "There is surely a future hope for you, and your hope will not be cut off" (Prov. 23:18).
- "But those who hope in the Lord will renew their strength. They will soar on wings like eagles; they will run and not grow weary, they will walk and not be faint" (Isa. 40:31).
- "Yet this I call to mind and therefore I have hope: Because of the Lord's great love we are not consumed, for his compassions never fail" (Lam. 3:21–22).
- "The Lord is good to those whose hope is in him, to the one who seeks him" (Lam. 3:25).
- "Not only so, but we also rejoice in our sufferings, because we know that suffering produces perseverance;

perseverance, character; and character, hope. And hope does not disappoint us, because God has poured out his love into our hearts by the Holy Spirit, whom he has given us" (Rom. 5:3–5).

- "Be joyful in hope, patient in affliction, faithful in prayer" (Rom. 12:12).
- "May the God of hope fill you with all joy and peace as you trust in him, so that you may overflow with hope by the power of the Holy Spirit" (Rom. 15:13).
- "I pray also that the eyes of your heart may be enlightened in order that you may know the hope to which he has called you, the riches of his glorious inheritance in the saints" (Eph. 1:18).
- "May our Lord Jesus Christ himself and God our Father, who loved us and by his grace gave us eternal encouragement and good hope, encourage your hearts and strengthen you in every good deed and word" (2 Thess. 2:16–17).
- "And the God of all grace, who called you to his eternal glory in Christ, after you have suffered a little while, will himself restore you and make you strong, firm and steadfast" (1 Pet. 5:10).

Your Chance to Dance:

- Think of one hardship or frustrating situation you're currently experiencing. Make a list of ways you could turn it into something positive.
- Make a list of fun things you enjoy doing. When immersed in hard times, commit to doing something on your "fun" list to give yourself a break.
- Make a copy of Charles Swindoll's quote regarding attitude, and read it often.
- Ask God daily to help you see His goodness around you. Begin each day with a prayer of thanksgiving.

APPENDIX

How do I secure my place in heaven for eternity?

God's desire is that none should perish, but that all would spend eternity with Him. However, because of His holiness and our sin, He created a way to cover our sins. Jesus is the only way to be joined to God. Becoming a Christian is seemingly simple but requires a distinct choice. We must believe that Jesus is the Son of God and that He died on the cross as a sacrifice for our sins. When we confess this to God and then ask forgiveness for our sins, God accepts us into His kingdom forever. Obviously, this is just the beginning step, because God desires a personal, ongoing relationship with each of us. The journey begins here. (See Romans 3:23; 6:23; 5:8; 10:8–10.)

ENDNOTES

Chapter One

1. *Merriam-Webster® Online Dictionary,* s.v. "Happiness," http://www.merriam-webster.com/dictionary/happiness.
2. Ibid.

Chapter Two

1. Helen H. Lemmel, "Turn Your Eyes Upon Jesus," 1922.

Chapter Three

1. *Merriam-Webster® Online Dictionary,* s.v. "Submit," http://www.merriam-webster.com/dictionary/submit.
2. Beth Moore, *Breaking Free: Making Liberty in Christ a Reality in Life* (Nashville: LifeWay, 1999), 129.
3. Dick Purnell, *Knowing God by His Names* (Eugene, Oregon: Harvest House, 2005), 91–107.

Chapter Four

1. Anna M Adachi-Mejia et al., "Children with a TV in their bedroom at higher risk for being overweight," *International Journal of Obesity* 31, no. 4 (2007): 644–51.

Chapter Five

1. "Religion an Introduction," http://religionencyclopedia. info/, October 25, 2009

Chapter Six

1. *Merriam-Webster® Online Dictionary,* s.v. "Grace," http:// www.merriam-webster.com/dictionary/grace.

Chapter Seven

1. Author unknown, accessed at http://www.heavensinspirations.com/silversmith.html, October 25, 2009.
2. Ernest Lehman, *The Sound of Music,* (20th Century Fox, 1965).

Chapter Ten

1. George Müller, as quoted in Bonnie Harvey, *George Müller: Man of Faith* (Uhrichsville, OH: Barbour Publishing, 1998) 152.
2. The Resiliency Center, "Definitions," http://www.resiliencycenter.com/definitions.shtml, accessed October 27, 2009.
3. Elizabeth Scott, "The Traits, Benefits, and Development of Emotional Resilience," http://stress.about.com/od/understandingstress/a/resilience.htm, accessed October 27, 2009.
4. Charles R. Swindoll, *Strengthening Your Grip* (Waco, TX: Word Books, 1982), 207.
5. Horatio Spafford, "It Is Well With My Soul," 1873.

Ashlynn Faith Shufflebarger
Our visitor from heaven and precious gift from God

Special thanks to Jessica Robertson

Jessica Robertson
Photographic Artistry